D0921533

Bond Book

This book is one of 155,000 in a special purchase to upgrade the CALS collection. Funds for the project were approved by Little Rock voters on 8/17/04.

Essential Histories

The Ottoman Empire
1326–1699

Essential Histories

The Ottoman Empire
1326–1699

Stephen Turnbull

OSPREY
PUBLISHING

First published in Great Britain in 2003 by Osprey Publishing,
Elms Court, Chapel Way, Botley Oxford OX2 9LP, UK
Email: info@ospreypublishing.com

ISBN 1 84176 569 4

Editorial by Ilios Publishing, Oxford, UK
(www.iliospublishing.com)
Design: Ken Vail Graphic Design, Cambridge, UK
Index by David Worthington
Cartography by The Map Studio
Origination by Grasmere Digital Imaging, Leeds, UK

04 05 06 10 9 8 7 6 5 4 3 2

A CIP catalogue record for this book is available from the
British Library.

For a complete list of titles available
from Osprey Publishing please contact:

Osprey Direct UK, PO Box 140,
Wellingborough, Northants, NN8 2FA, UK.
Email: info@ospreydirect.co.uk

Osprey Direct USA, c/o MBI Publishing, PO Box 1,
729 Prospect Ave, Osceola, WI 54020, USA.
Email: info@ospreydirectusa.com

www.ospreypublishing.com

Dedication
To Paul and Burcu Arrowsmith, on the happy occasion of
their wedding on 26 July 2003. This is the heritage they
both now share.

Acknowledgements
I would like to thank everyone who has assisted me with this
work, particularly the staff of museums in Turkey, Austria, Poland
and Hungary whose collections have special relevance to the
Ottoman conquests. Above all I thank my dear wife Jo, who
provided her customary administrative backup for one of her
last projects.

Editor's note
Unless otherwise indicated, all the images in this book are the
property of the author.

Contents

Introduction

In February of the year 1221 Tolui, the son of Genghis Khan, sat on a golden chair on a barren plain in present-day Afghanistan and watched the mass execution of the survivors of the Mongol capture of Merv. Men, women and children were herded together and given to the soldiers to be killed in batches of between two and three hundred each. It was shortly afterwards, according to tradition, that an Orghuz clan living nearby heard of the atrocities and emigrated to Asia Minor, where the Seljuks gave them land. These refugees were the founders of the Ottoman Empire.

The purpose of this book is to provide a concise, reliable and readable account of the wars of the Ottoman Empire. As the foundation and maintenance of the Ottoman hegemony was such an enormous undertaking in space as well as time this book will concentrate on the period between the establishment of the Ottoman capital at

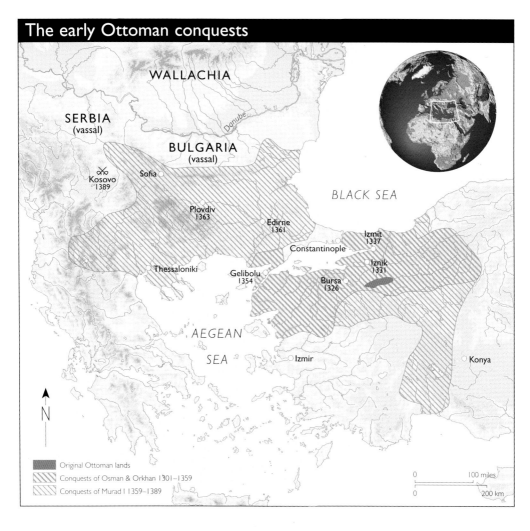

The early Ottoman conquests

WALLACHIA

SERBIA
(vassal)

Danube

BULGARIA
(vassal)

Kosovo
1389

Sofia

BLACK SEA

Plovdiv
1363

Edirne
1361

Izmit
1337

Constantinople

Iznik
1331

Thessaloniki

Gelibolu
1354

Bursa
1326

AEGEAN
SEA

Izmir

Konya

N

Original Ottoman lands

Conquests of Osman & Orkhan 1301–1359

Conquests of Murad I 1359–1389

0   100 miles

0   200 km

Bursa in 1326 and the Peace of Karlowitz in 1699. Limitations of space also require a concentration on the Ottoman confrontations with the West, although the important repercussions arising out of campaigns against Egypt and Persia will also be examined.

The city of Istanbul, as Constantinople the capital of the Byzantine Empire and from 1453 the capital of the Ottoman Empire. This view is taken looking across the Golden Horn from the Galata Tower.

Chronology

1301 Osman attacks Nicaea (Iznik)
1326 Orkhan captures Brusa (Bursa)
1329 Nicaea is finally captured
1337 Nicomedia (Izmid) is captured
1345 Annexation of the *beylik* of Karasi
1346 Ottomans form an alliance with John Cantacuzenus
1352 Ottomans capture Tzympe (Chimenlik)
1354 An earthquake allows the Ottomans to occupy Gallipoli (Gelibolu)
1361 Capture of Adrianople (Edirne)
1362 Accession of Murad I
1363 Capture of Philippopolis (Plovdiv)
      First battle of the Maritza
1365 Edirne becomes the new Ottoman capital
1371 Battle of Samakov
      Battle of Cernomen
      Second battle of the Martiza (Sirpsindigi)
1385 Ottomans enter Albania
      Capture of Sofia
1386 Capture of Nis
1387 Capture of Thessalonica
      Capture of Konya
1389 Battle of Kosovo
1393 Collapse of Bulgarian independence
1396 Battle of Nicopolis
1402 Battle of Ankara
1422 Siege of Constantinople
1444 Battle of Varna
1448 Second battle of Kosovo
1453 Conquest of Constantinople
1456 Siege of Belgrade
1462 Ottoman invasion of Wallachia
1475 Battle of Vaslui
1480 Ottoman invasion of Italy
1480 First siege of Rhodes
1492 Battle of Villach
1500 Capture of Modon
1514 Battle of Tchaldiran

1516 Capture of Aleppo
      Capture of Damascus
1517 Capture of Cairo
1520 Accession of Suleiman the Magnificent
1521 Capture of Belgrade
1522 Second siege of Rhodes
1526 Battle of Mohacs
1529 Siege of Vienna
1532 Siege of Güns (Koszeg)
1552 Siege of Erlau (Eger)
1565 Siege of Malta
1566 Siege of Szigeth (Szigetvar)
      Death of Suleiman the Magnificent
1570 Conquest of Cyprus
1571 Battle of Lepanto
1574 Capture of Tunis
1593 Thirteen Years War begins against Hungary
1594 Capture of Raab (Gyor)
1595 Austrians capture Gran (Esztergom)
1596 Ottomans take Erlau (Eger)
      Battle of Kerestes
1598 Loss of Raab (Gyor)
1600 Capture of Kanizsa (Nagykanicsa)
1601 Loss of Stuhlweissenburg (Szekesfehervar)
1606 Peace of Zsitva-Torok
1620 Battle of Cecora
1621 Battle of Chocim
1645 Invasion of Crete
1656 Battle of the Dardanelles
      Mehmet Koprulu becomes Grand Vizier
1676 Ahmed Koprulu becomes Grand Vizier
1664 Battle of St Gottard
1669 Capture of Crete
1676 Kara Mustafa becomes Grand Vizier
1683 Siege of Vienna
1686 Loss of Buda
1687 Second battle of Mohacs
1688 Loss of Belgrade
1697 Battle of Zenta
1699 Treaty of Karlowitz

The rise of the Ottomans

Hulegu Khan, the son of Tolui and grandson of Genghis Khan, died in 1265. His successors were the Ilkhans of Persia, who embraced both Islam and civilisation with equal enthusiasm. As the historian Rashid ad-Din puts it, 'the Mongols, who until then had only destroyed, now began to build'. But the price of this civilisation was the abandonment of the harsh Mongol heritage leading to consequences warned about by Genghis Khan, and in 1291 a succession dispute among the Ilkhans of Persia plunged their outlying territories into a state of anarchy. Frontier wars with Mamluk Egypt began while rebellions broke out in Asia Minor, where the slow collapse of the Seljuk kingdom, weakened by Mongol inroads, encouraged certain petty rulers to stake their claims to independence. Among these opportunists in north-west Anatolia were the former refugees called the Ottomans, who had originally controlled only a few square miles of pasture and farmland as vassals of the Seljuks.

The political situation in Anatolia was changing rapidly in another way, because as the Seljuk kingdom had begun to break up a different manifestation of militant Islam had risen to power. This was the aggressive fanaticism of independent bands known as *ghazis*, groups of 'holy warriors' who fought to spread the faith and supported themselves through plunder. Without tribal or territorial basis, the *ghazis* attached themselves to any outstanding leader who promised victory. Such leaders then tended to establish themselves by degree as the lords of the territories they had conquered. The early Ottomans were typical *ghazis*.

The wider world into which the Ottoman Empire was to be born was also undergoing immense change. The northern shores of the Mediterranean between the Bosphorus and

Granada were almost entirely in Christian hands, while its southern coast fell under the Islamic sphere of influence. The eastern flank was dominated by the Mamluk sultans of Egypt. The south and west coasts of Asia Minor formed different Muslim lands apart from the tiny enclaves such as Rhodes that were the heirs of the crusading kingdoms. To the north was the ancient but still powerful Byzantine Empire and its as yet insignificant Muslim neighbours the Ottomans.

The territory of the Ottomans was originally the smallest of the Turkish emirates in western Anatolia. It was also the nearest of all the *ghazi* lands to mighty Constantinople, capital of the great Byzantine Empire. This proximity to Byzantine lands meant that when they began to expand the Ottomans faced greater resistance compared to other *ghazi* movements. But relations with the Byzantine Empire also gave their leader Osman the time to build up the social and political structures that would sustain the new acquisitions that his sword had won. His location too, near ancient and well-established trade routes that no rebellion could erase, put the Ottomans in touch with great traditions of civilisation and good government that would help them flourish in the centuries to come.

The first Ottoman advance

The first expansion by the Ottoman emirate was made at the expense of its Turkish neighbours in Anatolia. An important development took place in 1291. When a succession dispute for the Mongol Ilkhanate broke out in Persia the Anatolian Turcomans

Soldiers of the Ottoman Empire fighting European knights.

rebelled and the *emir* Yavlak Arslan was killed. His son Ali took revenge, but then renounced his allegiance to the Seljuks and their Mongol overlords. Ali went on to attack Byzantine territory, but after some fighting established peaceful relations with the Christian state. His neighbour to the south, the Ottoman *ghazi* called Osman, was not so peacefully inclined and when Ali made peace with the Byzantines Osman took over the leadership of the raids. Other *ghazis* were attracted by his success, and by 1301 Osman was knocking on the gates of Nicaea (Iznik). The Ottoman conquests were about to begin.

By this time Osman already controlled a territory stretching from Dorylaeum (Eskisehir) to Brusa (Bursa). Before long the Byzantine Emperor dispatched an army against Osman, but Osman ambushed and destroyed it at Baphaeum (Koyunhisar), forcing the local population to flee to Nicomedia (Izmit) while other Ottoman forces approached Brusa. He finally succeeded in capturing Melangeia (Yenishehir), an act that cut communications between Brusa and Nicaea.

The victories around Nicaea made Osman famous, and thousands of immigrant Turkish households flocked to his standard. As a result the Byzantine Emperor Andronicus II became so concerned by the Ottoman threat that he sought alliances. A deal was struck with the Persian Ilkhan Oljeitu, to whom the emperor offered his sister in marriage. As a result of this arrangement a force of Mongols invaded the Ottoman district of Eskisehir, where they were soundly beaten by Osman's son Orkhan. The Ottomans were triumphant. The old Seljuk kingdom had

A sipahi *and a* Janissary.

ceased to exist in 1302 and the Ilkhanate was in disarray, so there was little to stop any further Ottoman moves against the Byzantine Empire. Wars and raiding continued, and shortly after Osman's death in 1326 Orkhan captured Brusa (Bursa), which became the first Ottoman capital. It is from this event that historians commonly date the founding of the Ottoman Empire and the beginning of a long process of military conquest.

By 1330 Emperor Andronicus III was compelled to acknowledge the initial Ottoman conquests. But the advance did not stop there, and the emperor lost Nicaea (Iznik) to them in 1331. Then Nicomedia (Izmit) fell in 1337, and by annexing the beylik of Karasi in 1345 the Ottomans found themselves facing Europe for the first time. Orkhan appointed his son Suleiman bey of Karasi, from where he intended to extend his conquests into the Balkans. The whole south coast of the Sea of Marmara and the Asiatic shore of the Dardanelles were now in Ottoman hands.

The next moves by the Ottomans were helped immeasurably by the weakness of the Byzantine Empire. In 1342 civil war broke out between the supporters of the boy emperor John V Palaeologus (1341–71) and his rival the Regent John (later John VI) Cantacuzenus. In the early years of the struggle John Cantacuzenus made use of the soldiers of the ghazi leader Umur Bey. But when Umur Bey's base at Izmir was raided in 1344 he was no longer able to send troops to John Cantacuzenus. Umur Bey recommended as an alternative his ally Orkhan, and when the rebel emperor accepted the idea the Ottomans were placed centre stage in the affairs of the Byzantines.

A toehold in Europe

Orkhan seized the opportunity to form a strong alliance with John Cantacuzenus, and even went to the extent of marrying his daughter in 1346. Six thousand Ottoman troops were provided for the rebel cause, and shortly afterwards the Regent Cantacuzenus became Emperor John VI. He held the throne for eight years, supported by his loyal Ottoman allies, who spent most of their time holding off attacks from Serbia. When his ally Umur Bey died in 1348 Orkhan became the unquestioned leader of the Muslim forces at this vital edge of the Byzantine Empire. By the following year 20,000 Ottomans were actively engaged in Byzantine warfare, all the while making themselves utterly familiar with the highways and byways to which they would one day return on their own behalf.

In 1352 a new contest began for the Byzantine imperial throne when John V Palaeologus attempted to win back what he had lost. Orkhan was again called in to help John Cantacuzenus. In command of the army was his son Suleiman, whose operations took him as far as Adrianople (Edirne) in Thrace. On his way there he captured Tzympe (Chimenlik) on the isthmus of Gallipoli (Gelibolu), where he established a Turkish military post. This greatly alarmed his ally John VI Cantacuzenus, because the occupation of Tzympe looked a far more permanent affair than the customary mercenaries' camp. Negotiations began for Tzympe's return to the Byzantines after payment of a large sum of money, but nature intervened just as an agreement seemed to have been reached. In 1354 a large earthquake knocked down the walls of several nearby towns. The Ottoman troops rushed to seize the places as their terrified inhabitants fled to safety. What nature had given them they were determined to secure.

Gallipoli (Gelibolu) thus became the Ottomans' toehold in Europe, and soon their occupation spread to the surrounding lands. Mosques, schools and Muslim lawcourts began to appear. Orkhan also sought allies who could strengthen his position, of whom the most significant were the Genoese. Back in Constantinople John VI Cantacuzenus was blamed for allowing the situation to develop in the Ottomans' favour and was forced to renounce his throne.

Suleiman, who had taken the Turks into Europe, died in 1357 following a fall from his horse, while his father Orkhan died in 1359. He had survived all but one of his sons, who became Sultan Murad I and reigned until his death at the battle of Kosovo in 1389. Murad I stepped successfully into his brother's conquering shoes and after consolidating his position in Asia Minor won an important victory when he captured Adrianople in 1361. This city, renamed Edirne, was later to become the new Ottoman capital. The newly captured lands were settled with immigrants from Anatolia.

Murad also demonstrated how easily Constantinople could be outflanked by marching eastwards to the Black Sea. The current Byzantine Emperor, John V Palaeologus, could only look on helplessly from the walls of Constantinople as his capital was surrounded. In desperation he signed a treaty with Murad I. It guaranteed his safety but made the emperor into practically an Ottoman vassal. But in contrast to his humiliation the nearby Balkan states were preparing for war against the Ottomans. So from Edirne the Turks moved upstream in 1363 to capture Philippopolis (Plovdiv) with its valuable rice fields. It was an important, yet isolated, frontier base, but it brought the growing power of the Ottomans close to the sphere of influence of Serbia.

The Serbian challenge

While the Ottomans had been expanding out of Anatolia a different force had been growing in the north to challenge the Byzantine Empire. In 1331 Stephen Dushan ascended the throne of Serbia and spent the next 20 years building up a Serbian Empire. Just like the Ottomans Dushan had taken full advantage of the Byzantine succession dispute to conquer much of Albania as well as parts of Thrace and Macedonia. In 1346 he had himself crowned 'Emperor of the Serbs and Greeks', and invited the Venetians to join him in the conquest of Constantinople. Rumours that he was interested in reuniting the Catholic and Orthodox confessions

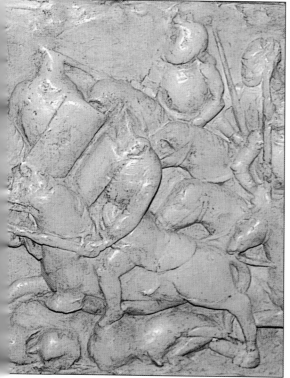

ABOVE A restored section of the land walls of Constantinople, showing them as they would have been seen by the Ottoman besiegers in 1396, 1422 and 1453.

LEFT The Ottomans in action against John Hunyadi, Hungary's great hero.

ensured Papal support for the scheme, but in 1355, just as he was about to set off on a grand crusade, Stephen Dushan died.

Dushan's Serbian Empire rapidly started to crumble after his death, but when the Ottomans occupied Philippopolis in 1363 there was sufficient glory left in the Serbian name to persuade its defeated commander to seek help from that direction. A united force of Serbs, Bosnians and Wallachians joined a Hungarian army under the Hungarian king, Louis the Great, and marched against the Turks at Edirne. But their rapid advance made the crusaders lazy. Less than two days from Edirne they made camp on the banks of the river Maritza and celebrated their progress with feasting. The local Ottoman commander led his predominantly light

The site of the battle of Ankara 1402, looking from the ancient city walls.

cavalry arm in an ambush by night. The Christians fled across the Maritza, which was in spate, and thousands drowned.

In 1365 the Sultan transferred his capital from Bursa to Edirne, a move of tremendous significance. To locate one's capital on the edge of one's territory next to hostile neighbours was an act of enormous self-confidence, and it proclaimed the sultan's future intentions with profound clarity. Edirne was also a natural centre of horse-breeding and soon became the seat of the imperial stables and stud-farms for the cavalry. Long after the capture of Constantinople it remained a favourite imperial residence.

From Edirne Murad I could look out over his territory as far as the coast of the Black Sea, a stretch of land that encircled the rapidly decreasing area dependent upon Constantinople. The toehold in Europe established at Gelibolu had now been replaced by a mighty presence and a dramatic statement of intent. The Ottoman advance could now continue from a firm base. The greatest phase of the conquests was about to start.

The Ottoman Army

Years earlier, when the state of the Anatolian Seljuks had developed into a fully formed Islamic sultanate, three border areas had been identified as marcher lands that could be more easily defended if fanatical Muslim *ghazis* were allowed to operate there. In the south such *ghazi* raids were directed against the Christian lands of Lesser Armenia and Cyprus. In the north the main effort was made against the Christian empire of Trebizond (Trabzon). The western marches, where the Ottomans emerged, lay along the Byzantine frontier.

The marches were wild frontier lands where nomads driven there by the Seljuks and refugees from the Mongol conquests came together to seek a better life. In each of these areas Seljuk interests were maintained by a hereditary *emir* (commander) of the marches. The main military strength within the marches, however, lay with the Turcoman tribes under their own *beys* (leaders), who were linked to the *emirs* through bonds of personal loyalty. These were nonetheless unstable organisations that could dissolve and re-form under up-and-coming *ghazis*. To the chroniclers of the Seljuk state such men were useful but unreliable robber barons prone to rebellion at a moment's notice.

The Ottoman *beylik* was one among several principalities that prospered initially at the expense of their Byzantine neighbours. Their new lands were strictly speaking part of the marches that came under the successive jurisdiction of the local *emir*, the Seljuk sultans and the Mongol Ilkhans. In reality, however, the *ghazi beys* regarded themselves as being independent in the former Byzantine territories that they had conquered.

The *ghazi* warriors who fought for Osman provided the nucleus of what was to become

the army of the Ottoman Empire. Some had once been tribal leaders. Others had been *emirs* under the Seljuk sultans, but what all of them had in common was a fanatical devotion to Islam and a commitment to extending Muslim influence through warfare. They had plenty of opportunity for this because the borders were so unstable. According to the historian Oruj, the Ottomans were:

Ghazis *and champions striving in the way of truth and the path of Allah, gathering the fruits of* ghaza *and expending them in the way of Allah, choosing truth, striving for religion, lacking pride in the world, following the way of the Sharia, taking revenge on polytheists, friends of strangers, blazing forth the way of Islam from the East to the West.*

The Ottoman Empire lived for war. Every governor in this empire was a general and every policeman was a *Janissary*. Every mountain pass had its guards and every road had a military destination. It was a commitment that stretched to the very top of Ottoman society. At the siege of Baghdad in 1683, when the Persians demanded that the contest be decided by single combat, Sultan Mehmet IV took on the task himself and killed the Persian champion. 'For this I was born, to bear arms,' said Bayezid the Thunderbolt, and when a European visitor got the chance to see Mehmet the Conqueror's army in the field in 1462 he surmised that such splendid troops could conquer all of Europe if they chose.

As the empire expanded the 'marches' of the Ottoman lands moved to the Balkans, where marcher traditions similar to the old patterns soon developed. The expression *ghazi* gave way to *akinji* (raiders), who tended to be volunteers from Anatolia drawn to the

ABOVE The armour of a *sipahi*.

RIGHT The battle of Varna 1444. The victorious
Ottomans look down on the body of King Wladislaw III.
On the left the treaty that the Christians broke is flown
from a spear.

frontier lands by the prospect of gaining a
timar (fief), for themselves. The *akinji* were
used by the Ottomans as an auxiliary militia
for intelligence gathering in enemy territory.
Renegade Christians were often recruited
into their ranks.

The *akinji* usually set off on a raid each
equipped with two horses, and were
organised in units of tens, hundreds and
thousands. As the Ottoman light cavalry the
akinji carried a sword, a shield, a scimitar a
lance and a mace. Leaders called *sanjak bey*
(provincial leaders) commanded them. Casual

raiding became a less frequent occupation
as the empire grew and by the time of the
battle of Mohacs in 1526, the *akinji* were
well accustomed to being employed for
penetrating enemy territory ahead of the
main Ottoman Army. They would secure
bridges and take prisoners for interrogation.

The *akinji* bands roamed far and wide,
and never were they more enthusiastic than
when they marched with the Sultan in the
vanguard of his army as they hoped to be
rewarded for their skill by promotion to the
ranks of the regular army. It was every

horseman's dream to enrol in the permanent army and receive the stipend known as a *timar* that would free him from economic worries and allow him to concentrate on war. He would then also be the recipient of a certain number of imperial taxes himself, even though the Ottoman Sultan owned all the land. In one particularly bloody assault a single *timar* was awarded and then re-awarded eight times after the previous recipients died fighting. At the siege of Belgrade the *Janissaries* stormed the walls over a moat filled with dead *akinji*.

The famous *Janissaries* were the elite of the Ottoman Army and for centuries were ranked among the finest infantry in Europe. They were originally recruited exclusively from the products of a system whereby Christian boys of between about eight and 15 years of age were selected from the conquered territories as 'tribute children'. They were trained in Turkish speech and customs and converted (often willingly) to Islam. After a period of intense physical training they were drafted into either the army or government posts according to their abilities. In the former case

The fortress of Rumeli Hisar, which proved decisive in cutting off seaborne relief to Constantinople in 1453.

they filled the ranks of the *Janissaries*, whose status as 'slave soldiers' is totally misleading in view of the high office that was open to them and the immense trust placed in them.

Some *Janissary* units provided the Sultan's bodyguard. At the battle of Varna in 1444 the formidable *Janissaries* occupied the centre positions with a ditch around them. Behind them stood the camels, while further behind was a breastwork of shields fixed to the ground in front of the other *Janissaries* who guarded the Sultan.

It is worth noting the additional presence in the marches of the *sipahis* (free cavalrymen) who were loyal to the local *bey*.

Roman times – paid, fed and unleashed through unsurpassable feats of organisation. When they marched on Persia in 1548 they were so well provisioned that they could cheerfully ignore the scorched earth landscape created by the Shah. Nowhere was their organisation better displayed than in camp. Western military camps were babels of disorder, drunkenness and debauchery. The Ottoman camps were disturbed by nothing louder than the sound of a mallet on a tent peg. 'I think there is no prince', wrote the chronicler Chalkondylas, 'who has his armies and camps in better order, both in abundance of victuals and in the beautiful order they use in encampment without any confusion or embarrassment.' Also, while western rulers needed to cajole or threaten their vassals the Ottoman armies assembled like clockwork. Their transport camels gave them a keen logistical advantage and the Ottomans always carefully analysed the problems of war. Each winter the previous year's campaigns were subject to a stringent post-mortem enhanced by reports from a network of spies. Weaknesses would be noted and plans made for the coming year.

The *sipahis* were invariably Muslim Turks. They were scattered across the empire, always on the move from billet to billet, and from billet to the front line. Even madmen had their own regiment: the *deli*, or maniacs, the 'riskers of souls' who allowed themselves to be used as human battering rams.

The Ottomans were the first state to maintain a standing army in Europe since

The advance against Europe 1365–1402

Into Bulgaria

The establishment of Edirne as the Ottoman capital in 1365 was a statement of intent to the inhabitants of the Balkans and the Ottoman conquest now began in earnest with differing Christian reactions to it. For example, Ragusa (Dubrovnik), which was unprotected from the advancing Ottomans, sought accommodation by treaties and signed an agreement with the Sultan to guarantee the safe continuation of its commercial activities. Other rulers were more devious in their relations with the Ottomans.

The arrival of the Turkish Army before Constantinople in 1453, from an exterior wall paiting on the monastery at Moldovita, Romania. (David Nicolle)

In 1365 one of the heirs of Bulgaria, dissatisfied with his share of his father's lands, sought Turkish help against his brother Shishman. But before the Turks could intervene the Hungarians invaded Bulgaria. It was therefore most unfortunate that at the end of the same year the Byzantine Emperor should choose to pass through Bulgaria en route to Buda. The Bulgarians kidnapped him in Vidin and prevented him from returning to Constantinople.

In 1366 the Pope proclaimed a crusade to expel the Turks from the Balkans, but the only ruler to respond was the captive Byzantine emperor's cousin Duke Amadeus VI of Savoy, who took his fleet through the Aegean to the Dardanelles. There he recaptured Gallipoli (Gelibolu), which was

an important prize indeed, but Amadeus was probably more satisfied when a show of force liberated John V from his genteel Bulgarian captivity. This further weakened the Bulgarian leadership, plunging Shishman into a disadvantageous agreement with Sultan Murad I. The alliance did not last, and with the battle of Samakov in 1371 Bulgarian independence was effectively at an end.

The road to Kosovo

When Stephen Dushan of Serbia died his empire passed into the hands of his young son Urosh. His vassals soon renounced their allegiance to him and set themselves up as independent princes. One of these Serb leaders, Vukashin, who ruled in Serres, combined his forces with sympathetic Serbian allies and marched northwards towards the Maritza Valley full of hope. But far from driving the Turks out of Europe they suffered a great defeat on 26 September 1371 at the battle of Cernomen where all the Serbian leaders were killed. This battle, also known as the second battle of the Maritza, was called in the Turkish chronicles 'Sirf sindigi' (the destruction of the Serbs). Murad I was prudent after his victory and left much of Macedonia and Serbia in the hands of local chiefs as his vassals. They included a certain Lazar, who, although connected with the Dushan family did not claim the royal title.

Almost ten years went by before the Turkish advance against Serbia was renewed. In the meantime they struck at Albania and Bulgaria. So confused had been the state of Albania that its rulers were used to calling in foreign troops to aid them against internal rivals, and so it was that the lord of Durazzo called upon the Ottomans as allies in 1385. The price was vassaldom and when the fortresses of Croia and Scutari fell to Murad I he handed them over to his loyal Albanian followers. Elsewhere Thessalonica surrendered in 1387, but Murad I also sought to consolidate his position in Anatolia and took Konya from the Turkish house of Karaman that same year.

Lazar of Serbia seems to have been stung into action by the loss of Sofia in 1385, a defeat that was followed in 1386 by the occupation of the Serbian city of Nis. He was also embarrassed by the use of Serbian vassal troops in the Ottoman Army, so a combined force of Serbs and Bosnians went to war and defeated the local Turkish commander. The victorious army grew, swollen in number by hopeful contingents from Bulgaria, Wallachia, Albania and Hungary. But swift action by Murad I detached Bulgaria from the league and, as he marched north to take on Lazar, he was joined by many sympathetic Serbian nobles.

The resulting armed clash was the famous battle of Kosovo, fought in June 1389, an encounter that still has tremendous significance in Balkan politics today. Among all the legends about the battle and its aftermath three facts stand out. The Ottoman Turks were victorious; Murad I was killed by a Serb at some point, although not during the actual fighting; and Lazar of Serbia was captured and executed in revenge. His son Stephen Lazarevic succeeded him and reigned for many years as a loyal Turkish vassal.

The victories of Bayezid the Thunderbolt 1389–96

Murad's son Bayezid I, who is known to history by the splendid appellation of 'the Thunderbolt', immediately succeeded the dead victor of Kosovo. Murad was the first Ottoman ruler to adopt the title of Sultan, a status confirmed solely by his military prestige, but Beyazid assumed the role in a new legal sense as the legitimate wielder of power in his domains. He was the most ambitious of the Ottoman leaders thus far. The confident Bayezid also diverged from the policy of his ancestors in his determination to wage war on rival Turkish principalities in Anatolia as vigorously as he did against infidels. He also alarmed an Italian trade delegation by boasting of his intention to conquer Hungary and Italy and to water his horse at the altar of St Peter's in Rome.

Such far reaching plans required a secure base, so Bayezid I began his military career with a series of operations to confirm Ottoman influence and domination in Anatolia and the Balkans. The first was needed because of revolts occasioned by the news of the death of Murad I at Kosovo. Bayezid dealt with his rivals with great efficiency and annexed what remained of the *ghazi beyliks* of western Anatolia.

In the Balkans matters went slowly but steadily. Bosnia held out until 1391. Bulgaria fought on until 1393, aided by Sigismund of Hungary. His was a cynical intervention that ended rapidly when he withdrew the Hungarian Army to escape entrapment. Soon the final spark of Bulgarian independence had burned out and in 1395 Bayezid turned his attentions for the first time directly against the greatest prize that both awaited and taunted the growing Ottoman Empire: the Byzantine capital of Constantinople.

The battle of Nicopolis 1396

The capital of the Byzantine Empire was a formidable place. Bayezid did not expect to bring down the mighty walls of Constantinople by attack, so instead he blockaded it from the straits, hoping to starve it out in time. That same year Bayezid also defeated Mircea of Wallachia, who fled to Hungary where he implored King Sigismund for help. The ultimate result was the great expedition and battle of Nicopolis, the first encounter between the Ottomans and troops from western Europe.

Mircea's aim was to regain his throne of Wallachia, Sigismund's was the saving of Hungary (Bayezid's earlier threats had been well disseminated). However, to the nobles of Europe who joined in the campaign that ended at Nicopolis the great expedition was nothing less than a crusade. The chief allies were Hungary, the Pope, the Duke of Burgundy and some leading French nobles. There was also a German and an English contingent. The plan was simple: a direct march to save the city of Constantinople, which was under a blockade by Bayezid I.

The crusaders assembled at Buda and marched down the line of the Danube, crossing at the Iron Gates in an operation that took an entire week. Once on soil ruled by Orthodox Christianity the army disgraced itself by looting and pillaging as its ancestors had during the notorious Fourth Crusade in 1204. Two Bulgarian towns fell to their advance, and then they reached their first real challenge: the fortified city of Nicopolis (Nikopol). But the confident crusaders had come without siege engines and as they sat helplessly before the city walls martial ardour was gradually replaced by indiscipline. Merry jousts were held, safe in the erroneous knowledge that Bayezid I was in Egypt. He was in fact near the still-blockaded Constantinople, and his subsequent swift and secret advance against Nicopolis fully justified his nickname.

In spite of the account by Froissart, who depicted the French knights being surprised in their tents, Bayezid the Thunderbolt did not attack the Christian camp but set up battle lines on ground of his own choosing in territory that was already very familiar to him. His dispositions made use of ravines on the flanks and also allowed the Turkish rearguard to be concealed on the reverse slope. Among these concealed troops were Serbian horsemen under Stephen Lazarevic.

The delay allowed the Christian Army to formulate its own plans of attack. King Sigismund wanted to send forward his Hungarian mounted archers to test the mettle of the Ottoman light cavalry screen before following up with the heavier armed knights of Hungary and Europe. This plan was supported by Mircea of Wallachia, but drew opposition from the visiting crusaders, as it did not suit their martial pretensions. Ignoring the need for cooperation, the French knights advanced in good order ahead of their allies, determined to strike the first blow against the infidel.

The attack was a disaster. King Sigismund and his Hungarians did not engage in the centre, something that led to the French accusing them of treason. However, the king only became aware of their probable fate when

A typical Ottoman battle.

a stampede of wounded and riderless horses swept by him. The Hungarians then advanced to engage the victorious Ottomans, but Bayezid's reserve troops, Stephen Lazarevic's Serbs, clinched the victory as they charged in and caused havoc. The crusader army broke and fled back to the flotilla of galleys that had provided their support down the Danube. Chaos reigned as the defeated soldiers began fighting each other for a place on the boats.

Nicopolis was Bayezid's greatest victory, and was marred only by his execution of prisoners the following day. He was apparently irritated by the huge losses sustained by his victorious army, and when reports reached him of massacres elsewhere he replied in kind. Few were spared. Among the fortunate ones held for ransom was Jean de Nevers, the son of the Duke of Burgundy and the future 'John the Fearless', and a young man called Johann Schiltberger, who was saved on account of his age and lived to write his memoirs. Schiltberger describes the aftermath of Nicopolis thus:

Then each was ordered to kill his own prisoners, and for those who did not wish to do so the king appointed others in their place. Then they took my companions and cut off their heads, and when it came to my turn, the king's son saw me and ordered that I should be left alive, and I was taken to the other boys, because none under 20 years of age were killed, and I was scarcely 16 years old.

Disaster at Ankara

The huge Turkish victory at Nicopolis made the position of Constantinople look even more perilous than ever. The city did not fall to an Ottoman siege this time, but the loss of the allied army on the Danube made it less likely in future for any European prince to urge a crusade to save it. Nevertheless, in 1399 Emperor Manuel II went in person to plead his cause in the courts of Europe. His pleas for aid were eventually answered, but help came from an entirely unexpected direction.

The campaigns of Bayezid the Thunderbolt had consolidated his rule on both sides of the

A further section of the walls of Constantinople, laid low by the heavy artillery of Mehmet the Conqueror.

Bosphorus: the European and Balkan front known as Rumelia, and the Asian side of Anatolia. So successful had he been in the latter direction that his conquests had brought him into contact with another emerging power: that of the heir of the Mongols called Timur Lenk (Timur the Lame), known to the west as Tamberlane.

While Bayezid had triumphed in the western part of what is modern Turkey, Timur had staked an equally formidable claim in the east, capturing the strategic city of Sivas in 1400. Throughout his campaigns along the Anatolian marches and in Syria diplomatic exchanges had continued between Timur and the Christian lands nearby. These included the emperor of Trebizond (Trabzon), who feared the Ottomans more than Timur and hurried to send tribute. Nor had Timur neglected to

keep Bayezid I informed of his latest conquests, and the capture of Sivas was waved in front of his face as a taunt. Timur sought in particular the return from Bayezid's protection of certain dignitaries who had escaped the fall of Baghdad. Bayezid's response was to assemble his troops, drawing large numbers of vassal soldiers out of the Balkans and suspending the long siege of Constantinople just at the point when his blockade was beginning to show some effect. Envoys were sent to Timur and met him near Sivas. Timur made a grand show of reviewing his troops within sight of the envoys. The army included magnificently attired reinforcements recently sent from Samarkand.

Bayezid secured his rear by stationing nine ships at Gelibolu and another 20 in the Aegean. He then moved eastwards as quickly as possible to prevent a deep penetration of his territory by the enemy. His objective was the strategic city of Ankara, now Turkey's capital

Wounded Turkish soldiers at the siege of Belgrade, 1456, from a modern fresco in the 'mosque church' at Pecs, Hungary.

and already important owing to its position at the crossroads of the routes from Syria and Armenia. Summer was coming to an end and the crops were ready for harvesting, so it was a bad time to be going on campaign. The sultan rejected the advice of his councillors to wait for Timur near the well-watered region near Ankara. Instead he left a reserve garrison there and continued eastwards.

Timur was being kept informed of the Ottoman movements by scouts and he headed south-west from Sivas, following the curve of the Kizilirmak River. After six days of forced marches they reached Kayseri without meeting any opposition from Ottoman forces. They rested there for four days then rode for another four days across Cappadocia to the environs of Kirsehir, where the first armed contact was made with Ottoman scouts.

Three more days brought Timur's Army to the camping grounds to the north-east of Ankara that had recently been vacated by Bayezid. Timur gave orders for immediate

siege operations against Ankara's mighty Byzantine walls. The city's water supply was diverted and the mining of the ramparts began. Mongol troops were already scaling the walls when news came in that Bayezid had abandoned his march to Sivas and was two days away from Ankara.

When the Ottoman Army arrived they were in a very poor state. The only source of water available for Bayezid's troops was a spring that Timur had arranged to be fouled. They were therefore in no position to fall upon the rear of a besieging army, so Timur was given ample opportunity to organise his battle lines. They looked magnificent, being crowned at the front by the presence of war elephants from India.

Bayezid's Army included Serbian troops under his brother-in-law Stephen Lazarevic and the Serbs scored the first gain of the day by driving back Timur's left wing. But there were problems among the Ottoman ranks. Certain contingents from Anatolia were from a similar ethnic background to Timur's own troops and his agents had been active among them. At Ankara they were fighting their own kind, not Balkan Christians. Many of them recognised their former masters in the opposing ranks and came over to Timur's side. Faced by rear attacks along with the frontal assault the Ottoman Army began to give way. On the right wing Lazarevic's Serbs hung on until forced to retreat to cover other contingents'

Vlad Dracula the Impaler, Prince of Wallachia, whose favoured method of execution turned him into a legend.

withdrawal. Soon only Bayezid and his *Janissaries* were left. He held on until nightfall, then retreated with only 300 warriors left to accompany him. The enemy followed in hot pursuit and killed Bayezid's horse from under him.

In a dramatic end to a dramatic campaign Bayezid the Thunderbolt was taken prisoner and with him went Johann Schiltberger, the boy who had been spared at Nicopolis and had then entered the Sultan's service. Schiltberger gives us the best close-hand account of the last days of the great Sultan:

Weysit [Bayezid] took to flight, and went with at least 1,000 horsemen to a mountain. Temerlin surrounded the mountain so that he could not

move and took him. Then he remained eight
months in the country, conquered more territory
and occupied it … and he would have taken him
into his own country but he died on the way.

Other accounts tell how the city of
Ankara quickly submitted. Timur's Army
headed west hunting down the remnants
of Bayezid's Army. They finished by
plundering the vast wealth of Bursa,
including its magnificent bronze gates.
The extent of the disaster can be imagined
when one notes that Bayezid's son Suleiman
had to escape across the Sea of Marmara
on a Genoese galley. But far from
massacring the escaping Turks the citizens
of Constantinople generously helped ferry
them across the Bosphorus to freedom,
albeit for an enormous fee.

Bayezid the Thunderbolt was taken as a
captive across Anatolia and died in March
1403, probably at Timur's own hand. Timur's
Mongol Army devastated the Ottoman lands
as far as the Aegean and then laid siege to
Izmir, which had been won back from the
Turks in 1344 by the Knights of Rhodes. His
victory there ensured that Timur had
succeeded where his prisoner Bayezid had
failed and had extinguished the last
Christian outpost on the mainland. But
Timur had also captured the Sultan and
driven his son into exile. It appeared that
Timur the Lame had utterly destroyed the
Ottoman Empire.

Ottoman success 1422–1606

In the aftermath of the battle of Ankara the Ottoman Empire looked finished. Not only were the Turks beaten, but a power struggle broke out among the sons of Sultan Bayezid, a matter which was not resolved until 1411 with the accession of Mehmet I. As events were to prove, this was in fact a turning point in the Ottoman conquests and the beginning of their most successful period during which some of their most celebrated victories were won.

The 1422 siege of Constantinople

The Ottoman fortunes began to revive during the eight-year reign of Mehmet I, but it was not until the reign of his successor Murad II (1421–51) that serious moves were made against Christian territories in general and

The tower of St Nicholas in the harbour at Rhodes, the site of some of the fiercest fighting on the first siege of Rhodes in 1480.

Constantinople in particular. The 1422 siege of Constantinople was almost a dress rehearsal for the successful conquest of 1453. The latter operation has inevitably overshadowed the earlier conflict, but we are fortunate that an eyewitness called John Kananos left a vivid and exciting account of the campaign. Among the points that Kananos makes is a confirmation that siege artillery was being used by both sides during 1422 along with the more conventional medieval siege weapons. Siege towers pulled by teams of oxen are specifically mentioned.

The siege of Constantinople was abandoned in 1423. In 1424 a treaty was made with Byzantium that reduced its empire to little more than the city and, after fighting off local rebellions, Murad II felt able to restart his holy war. He marched on Macedonia, and captured Thessalonica in 1430. Albania was partly subdued between 1435 and 1436. These campaigns took Murad II very close to Hungary, whose great national hero John Hunyadi would soon be in arms against him.

The Hungarian campaign 1439–43

In 1439 Murad II captured the castle of Smederevo, which lay downstream from Belgrade. This caused George Brankovic, the Despot of Serbia, to become a refugee in Hungary. With Serbian support John Hunyadi launched a campaign against the commander of the Turkish Army occupying Smederevo, whom he caught off guard returning from a raiding party. The commander, Beg Iszhak, assumed that the Hungarians would adopt their usual tactics of attacking his main body with their mounted knights. Instead Hunyadi attacked them with dismounted men-at-arms while his horsemen encircled their enemy and attacked their flanks. The result was a considerable Hungarian victory, although Smederevo was not recaptured. To show his gratitude George Brankovic donated Belgrade to the Hungarian king.

In 1442 Murad II invaded Hunyadi's homeland of Transylvania. Hunyadi gave battle at Hermannstadt (Sibiu) and, later that same year, Murad II sent another army against Transylvania, but this time John Hunyadi waited for them close to his border at the narrow pass known as the Iron Gates. After attacking the *sipahis* and the *Janissaries* Hunyadi put into motion a false retreat, which lured the Turks back to the wagon line and, following a fierce fight, the Turks were defeated.

John Hunyadi had meanwhile appealed to the princes of western Europe to capitalise upon his victories and join him in a grand crusade against the Ottomans. Pope Eugenius IV supported him enthusiastically, but there was very little official response from the military leaders of Europe except for Poland, whose king Wladislaw III had been elected King of Hungary in 1439. We are however told that considerable numbers of French and German knights attended in a personal capacity as crusaders.

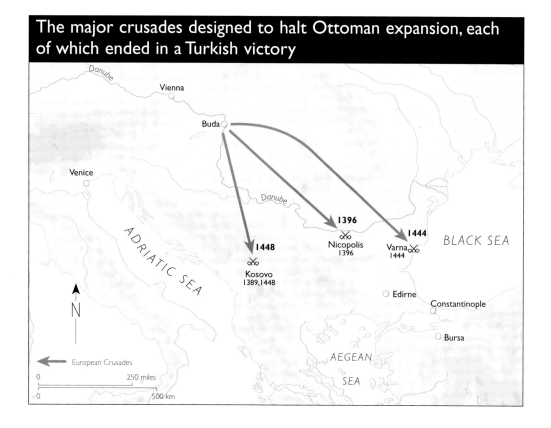

The major crusades designed to halt Ottoman expansion, each of which ended in a Turkish victory

The Yedikule fortress of Istanbul, added to the old walls of Constantinople at the Golden Gate.

The plan of campaign was uncomfortably like the humiliating Nicopolis crusade of 1396, but the 'Long Campaign' as it is known in Hungarian history began very successfully with a crossing of the Danube and a rendevous near Sofia, from where the army marched westwards and captured Nis on 3 November 1443. The Hungarians then crossed the Balkan mountains in winter and defeated a Turkish army. The objective was Philippopolis (Plovdiv) and to some it looked as though they could go much further and drive the Turks back across the Bosphorus, but after a victory on Christmas Day 1443 supplies were beginning to run low. Hunyadi sensibly withdrew and reached Buda in triumph in February 1444, where he received a hero's welcome. Murad II was forced to accept a ten-year truce with Hungary.

The battle of Varna 1444

The success of the Long Campaign brought messages of congratulation to John Hunyadi from all over Europe, and ideas of crusading began to be entertained once again – truce or no truce. At a Diet in Buda attended by the Papal Legate Cardinal Cesarini, a fanatic who once wrote that he could think day and night of nothing else other than the final ruin of the Turks, an ambitious plan was drawn up. A newly formed crusader army would follow the line of the Danube while Venetian ships prevented the Turks from crossing the straits and the Greeks made diversionary attacks in the Peloponnese. The Christians could then annihilate the 7,000 Turkish troops left in Thrace and Bulgaria and Constantinople would be saved. The recapture of Jerusalem was even discussed.

The plans were impressive, but soon began to fall apart. The Byzantine Emperor John VIII concluded that duplicity would not help his delicate relationship with the Sultan. He therefore refused to join in and, together with George Brankovic, prevented the Albanians from making any more positive a contribution. George Brankovic of Serbia, whose daughter was married to the Sultan, felt that he had more chance of regaining his territories through negotiation

In War abconterfaction
Mit namen Sultan Solleymon
Des Großmechtig Türckischen Keysers
Des Christentumbs starcken durchreyters.

Nwas gestalt/kleydung vnd sitte
Er ist in seinem heer geritten
Vor Wien in Ostrreich der Stat
Die er grausam belegert hat.

Ist dreimal hundert tausent man
Doch vnsighafftig zoch daruon
Durch Got der in daruon abschreckt
Ein ring jm in die nasen steckt.

Suleiman the Magnificent, the greatest of all the Ottoman leaders.

with his son-in-law than by force of arms. Terms were agreed in June 1444 whereby Brankovic received the return of several fortresses and hostages.

It looked as though the crusade would have to be cancelled, but Cardinal Cesarini persuaded the King of Hungary that an oath sworn to a Muslim was invalid, and when a Turkish delegation arrived in Szeged to ratify the earlier agreement, the king publicly reiterated his aim to 'hurl back the infidel sect

The mosque of Suleiman the Magnificent in Istanbul.

of Mahomet overseas'. He then marched into Bulgaria, but Murad II had been given ample time to complete his other campaigns in Asia Minor and prepare for a Christian attack.

Soon there was little more than a Hungarian army left to suffer the biggest crusading disaster since Nicopolis. Their one notable supporter was Vlad Dracula of Wallachia, who did not hesitate to express severe misgivings about the whole operation. He referred particularly to the meagre size of the Christian Army and warned King Wladislaw III that even the Sultan's hunting party contained more men than the crusading host. Then, one by one, the other elements in the grand plan started to collapse. The Greeks completed the supportive task allotted to them, but the Venetians were prevented by heavy winds from sealing off the Bosphorus. So instead of being confined to Asia Minor, Murad II was able to bribe the Genoese into transporting his army across to the European shore.

The two opposing forces met in battle near Varna on the Black Sea in November 1444. Hunyadi had chosen a strong position between the end of a marsh and the bay. Scouts brought news that the Turkish Army was scarcely 4,000 paces away and numbered at least 60,000 men. Cardinal Cesarini argued that they should make a defensive enclosure with the wagons, as had been done successfully in the past. Hunyadi was for launching an immediate attack, but his hand was forced by news that the Turks were already advancing, so the wagons were hastily arranged. The Wallachians took the left wing and the Hungarians took the right. King Wladislaw III, who was suffering from an abscess on his leg, was placed in the position of greatest safety in the centre where his Polish and Hungarian bodyguards surrounded him.

The Sultan pitched his tent on top of a hill, and legend tells that near to it he fixed the treaty of peace that the Hungarians had repudiated prominently on a pole. He had four soldiers for every one in the Hungarian Army. His Anatolian troops were on the left wing and his European troops were on the right. Just before the battle began a strong wind blew down all the Christian banners

A round tower in the land walls of Rhodes.

except for that of the king. This was inevitably taken as a bad omen, but the battle began well for them. Following an initial attack by Turkish mounted archers, a senior Turkish leader was killed during the first hand-to-hand encounter. Believing that victory was now assured, King Wladislaw III prepared to join the battle personally, something that John Hunyadi had tried to persuade him not to do.

Unlike the king, the experienced Hunyadi was not fooled into thinking that the Turks were already beaten, because as he travelled round the battlefield he could see that the crusader army was hard pressed at every point. At this point, according to the chronicler Chalkondylas, some knights near the king who were jealous of Hunyadi urged the young monarch to win some glory of his own and the next time Hunyadi returned to the royal command post his king had gone. Finding him enveloped within a cloud of *Janissaries*, Hunyadi attempted his rescue, but it was not long before the King of Hungary's head in its silver helmet was being waved on the point of a Turkish spear. From that moment on the crusaders were lost, but the battle had been so bloody and so evenly balanced up to that point that it was not until the following day that Murad II realised that he had won the greatest Turkish victory since Nicopolis.

The last victories of Murad II

Soon after the battle of Varna Murad II abdicated in favour of his son Mehmet, but certain problems forced the old Sultan back out of retirement. The most serious was John Hunyadi's Danube expedition of 1445. The Ottoman Army monitored and shadowed the raiders from the southern bank and by the end of the campaigning season in October Turkish pressure caused the new crusaders to withdraw.

Murad II made the next move when he returned to the Balkans to take further revenge for the treaty-breaking before Varna. The Greeks were the first to suffer for their support when the Peloponnese was captured in 1446, but at this point the newly elected

Pope Nicholas V proclaimed a new crusade. The Venetians fiercely opposed the scheme, and the only real support came from George Skanderbeg of Albania, who had once been a hostage of the Turks and was now a doughty fighter for his country.

The Ottoman response was an invasion of Albania and Murad II's incursions brought John Hunyadi back into the field. The Hungarians crossed the Danube into Serbia in September 1448 with the aim of linking up with Skanderbeg. Hunyadi led an army of 24,000 men, including 8,000 Wallachians, but suffered another military defeat without even seeing his Albanian allies. This encounter was the second battle of Kosovo, which was fought at the same site as the momentous struggle of 1389. Both sides were drawn up in an order similar to their dispositions at Varna, but, unlike Varna, there was no attempt made to break the Turkish line by a wild cavalry charge. Instead John Hunyadi set a strong force of German and Bohemian handgunners against the *Janissaries* in the Turkish centre with mounted knights on the flanks. As both sides acted defensively from behind field

The siege of Belgrade 1521.

fortifications the result was stalemate between the bullets from one side and the arrows and bolts from the other, and even an attack delivered under cover of darkness was insufficient to break the *Janissary* line. Meanwhile there was a series of cavalry charges on the wings until the Wallachian allies of Hunyadi gave way in the face of superior Turkish numbers on the second day.

Kosovo 1448 was Murad II's last great victory. He died in 1451, having failed to impose his rule only in Albania, where the national hero George Skanderbeg fought a fierce and successful guerrilla war against successive Ottoman armies. But the failure to take distant Albania was a trifling detail compared to what Murad II could now pass on to his successor Mehmet II, who was to earn the enviable sobriquet of Mehmet the Conqueror.

Mehmet the Conqueror 1451–81

Mehmet II was destined to become the greatest sultan of his line so far. Although young he had twice reigned in his father's stead and had accompanied him on

campaign. But in Europe he was widely believed to be a youth of no promise, weak and vicious, from whom nothing should be feared. His early acts were deliberately designed to foster these suspicions, because he desperately needed time to deal with domestic matters in Anatolia before embarking on his grand design.

As the year 1453 approached the Turks steadily tightened their grip on Constantinople, which was rapidly running out of allies. The current ruler of Wallachia was a Turkish vassal, as was George Brankovic of Serbia, who even sent troops to fight on the Turkish side during the great siege. The Knights Hospitaller of Rhodes were in no position to risk their island by sending military support, and the rulers of Morea, Georgia and Trebizond (Trabzon) were kept firmly in check. Ragusa (Dubrovnik) on the Dalmatian coast happily maintained its privileged position by paying an annual tribute to the Sultan and even John Hunyadi of Hungary, after his two defeats at Varna and Kosovo, had turned his thoughts from attack to defence. The result was that when the Byzantine Emperor John VIII passed away in October 1448 he died in the knowledge that Constantinople now stood alone, and that his successor would be isolated when he faced the greatest challenge in the empire's long history.

The conquest of Constantinople 1453

The conquest of Constantinople was a matter of vital concern to the Ottomans. At the meeting called by Mehmed II when it was decided to proceed with a campaign that was to end successfully in 1453, the following points were made:

1. The holy war, the *ghaza*, was the basic duty of the Ottoman *ghazis*.
2. The continued existence of Constantinople in the middle of the Ottoman Empire protected their enemies and incited them against the Sultan.
3. The Byzantine Empire had given sanctuary and support to false claimants to the Ottoman throne, and had been the main instigator of crusades.
4. There was every possibility that Constantinople could be surrendered to Latin Christendom. That would mean that the Ottoman Empire would never be fully integrated.

With these thoughts in mind preparations were made for war. Mehmet's long-term strategy of isolating the city from all sides continued with the taking of all the remaining Byzantine possessions on the Black Sea coast and, most important of all, he was determined to have full command of the sea. On the Asiatic shore of the Bosphorus lay a Turkish fortress called Anadolu Hisar. Mehmet now built another castle opposite it on the European side called Rumeli Hisar (the European castle). It was completed in August 1452 and allowed the Ottoman artillery to control all shipping in and out of the Black Sea in a way never before possible. In November 1452 a cannonball fired from Rumeli Hisar sank a Venetian galley. The days of relief armies arriving by sea were over.

In March 1453 an Ottoman fleet assembled off Gelibolu and sailed proudly into the Sea of Marmara while the Turkish Army assembled in Thrace. The sight of the Ottoman Navy passing under the sea walls of Constantinople towards Rumeli Hisar while the army approached its land walls was one that struck terror into the inhabitants. To add to the lesson already delivered from Rumeli Hisar concerning the potential of the Turkish artillery, there soon came lumbering into view a tremendous addition to their firepower. A well-known story tells how a Hungarian artillery expert named Urban approached the Byzantine Emperor with an offer to cast guns for the defence of the city. Because the price he demanded was too high he was sent away, so he immediately turned to the Sultan, who hired him for four times the fee he had asked. Urban boasted that these cannon could reduce 'even the walls of

The expansion of the Ottoman Empire under Mehmet the Conqueror

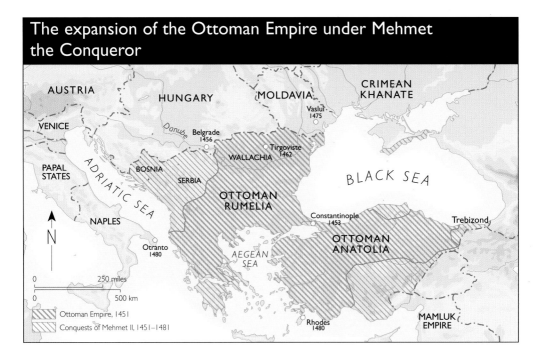

The crack in the side of the Bastion of St George at Rhodes was caused by the exploding of a mine during the siege of 1522.

Babylon'. They took three months to make and were test-fired at Edirne. The enormous cannon were each transported to Constantinople by 70 oxen and 10,000 men.

Following the advice of his artillerymen, Mehmet II positioned the siege guns against the weakest and most vulnerable parts of the wall. The targets included the imperial

The battle of Mohacs 1526, from a Turkish miniature on display in the castle of Szigetvar, Hungary.

palace of Blachernae at the north-western corner of the city and the Romanus Gate in the middle wall. The bombardment, which was to last 55 days, soon began to cause massive destruction. The defenders hit back with their own artillery weapons, but they faced several problems, one of the most serious being that the flat roofs of the towers in the medieval walls were not sufficiently strong to act as gun emplacements. As Leonard of Chios put it, 'the largest cannon had to remain silent for fear of damage to our own walls by vibration'. Chalkondylas even wrote that the act of firing cannon did more harm to the towers than the Turkish bombardment.

On 20 April three supply ships braved the Turkish blockade and entered the Golden Horn. This natural harbour, across which a stout chain had been slung, was the only sea area that the Byzantines still controlled. But two days later the defenders' elation turned to despair when Mehmet II put into motion an extraordinary feat of military engineering. A wooden roadway was constructed from the Bosphorus to a stream called the Springs that entered the Golden Horn, and with much muscular effort some 80 Turkish ships were dragged overland and relaunched far beyond the boom.

Seaborne attacks could now be made from much closer quarters, but rumours were heard concerning the approach of a relieving army from Hungary. This prompted Mehmet II to launch a simultaneous assault against the land and sea walls on Tuesday 29 May. The attack began in the early hours of the morning. The Byzantine emperor had concentrated his troops between the inner and middle walls and when they were in position the gates of the inner wall were closed because there was to be no retreat. The Turkish irregulars went in first but were driven back, as were the Anatolian infantry who followed them. A final attack by the *Janissaries* took the middle wall and when a wounded senior commander of Constantinople was seen being evacuated through the inner wall into the city the impression was given that he was retreating. Resistance began to fade and when the Emperor was killed in a brave counterattack Constantinople fell. The Ottomans had finally extinguished their most symbolic rival and the Ottoman Empire would never be the same again.

The siege of Belgrade 1456

Following the fall of Constantinople Hungary was surrounded by lands that were either sympathetic to the Ottomans or cowed by them. Skanderbeg's guerrillas in Albania were unlikely to leave their mountains and Serbia was equally passive, but owing to George Brankovic's earlier understanding with the Hungarians, the

state of Hungary now began at Belgrade. So in 1456 this mighty triple-walled fortress where the Sava met the Danube became the Mehmet the Conqueror's first objective in his post-Constantinople euphoria. 'I shall be dining peacefully in Buda within two months' he is reported as saying.

In the event Belgrade was saved by the citizens' army described below. But the rest of the Balkans still looked doomed and Serbia's neighbour, Bosnia-Herzegovina, also fell, but for very different reasons. The area had long been the heartland of the fiercely persecuted Bogomil sect, who saw in the Turks a probable relief from their sufferings, so many inhabitants welcomed the Ottomans. By the end of 1463 Bosnia had become another Ottoman dominion after the campaign described below through the eyes of Konstantin Mihailovic. Soon almost the whole Orthodox world of the Balkans was in Turkish hands, leaving only a small mountainous district later known as Montenegro to enjoy some measure of autonomy. In Albania George Skanderbeg repelled no less than 13 Turkish advances between 1444 and 1466 and it was only after his death in 1468 that the Turks were able to make any headway. In Greece the Duchy of Athens surrendered to the Turks in 1456 and internal dissensions made the Ottoman conquest of the Peloponnese a straightforward task. Only Hungary and its immediate neighbours now stood against the Turks.

The Ottoman war with Wallachia

In 1456 Wallachia, one of the Balkan principalities that had hitherto posed little threat to the growth of the Ottoman Empire, suddenly provided a new challenge. Taking advantage of the Sultan's concentration on the siege of Belgrade, Wallachia's exiled prince won back his throne and took an oath of suzerainty to the king of Hungary. By this

The castle of Güns (Koszeg), defended heroically against the Sultan in 1532.

The siege of Güns (Koszeg) in 1532.

act Wallachia finally repudiated any vestiges of loyalty it may have retained towards the Turks and placed itself on the front line against the Ottoman advance. Its previously obscure prince thereby began a new challenge to Mehmet's conquest. His name was Vlad Dracula and it was his war against Mehmet the Conqueror that made him a Balkan folk hero long before a 19th-century novelist appropriated his name for his classic gothic villain.

The real Vlad Dracula was no vampire, but certain aspects of his behaviour made him horrible enough. Without accepting all the tales of terror that are told about him, most of which were either elaborated or even invented by unsympathetic chroniclers long after his death, there is little ground for doubting that he employed torture as a weapon of statecraft. Dracula's notoriety derived largely from his favourite means of execution, so that he became known as Vlad Tepes (Vlad the Impaler).

Hostilities with the Ottomans began when Vlad Dracula refused to continue paying tribute to the Sultan and instead impaled the Turkish ambassadors. In 1461 he attacked and captured the fortress of Giurgiu and then led raids down the Danube in a campaign similar to Hunyadi's Long

Campaign of 1443, taking all the points along to the Danube Delta of the Black Sea from which the Turks could make a waterborne response. The chronicler Chalkondylas writes of Mehmet leading a Turkish army larger than any since the siege of Constantinople, outnumbering even the host sent against Belgrade. The force assembled at Philippopolis (Plovdiv) in May 1562, but because of Dracula's attacks on the Black Sea ports the Turkish naval involvement was minimal and they initially did little more than attack Brailla and Chilia near the Delta. The Turks then marched overland from Plovdiv and first tried to cross the Danube at Vidin, one of the few ports still left intact, but they were prevented by archery fire from disembarking on the far shore. Finally, during June, an advanced unit of Ottomans succeeded in landing at Turnu on the Romanian side of the river near Nicopolis.

Vlad's cruelty to Ottomans soldiers and civilians alike is described below. It was therefore in the Ottomans' favour that a resolution of the Wallachian campaign lay through the contrast that Mehmet was offering the people in the choice between Vlad and his brother Radu. Soon Vlad Dracula was on the run. After a few years of imprisonment he returned briefly to Wallachia, but was killed in battle in 1476.

The Moldavian campaign

Neighbouring Moldavia was ruled at the time by Stephen the Great, who put up a spirited resistance to the Ottoman advance. Mehmet II ordered an invasion of Moldavia in 1475, which was to be synchronised with an attack by sea against the Black Sea port of Chilia. Stephen concentrated his forces around Vaslui and the population of lower Moldavia fled to the mountains.

The Grand Vizier Suleiman led the Turkish advance and came upon a Moldavian covering force. The Moldavians gave way and slowly retreated, keeping up attacks on the Turkish columns. The state of the roads slowed the Ottomans down still further until they were successfully led towards the defensive position prepared by Stephen at Vaslui. The Ottoman vanguard arrived early on 10 January 1475. It was a dark and misty morning. Held up by the fierce fighting of the Moldavian troops the Ottomans were crushed by a counterattack led by Stephen the Great later in the day.

The Ottoman Army withdrew, but returned to Moldavia in 1476. This time the advance was supported by their vassal prince in Wallachia and from the north by the Tartars of the Ukraine. In view of the situation Stephen ordered the population of Moldavia to flee to the mountains, destroying crops and wells as they went. This made the Turkish advance very difficult and cholera soon added to their problems. Stephen attacked the vanguard at Valea Alba, but on the following day the Ottoman main body under Mehmet the Conqueror dispersed Stephen's guerrillas and began to overrun the country. Only an agreement with King Matthias Corvinus of Hungary promised help and when the Hungarians moved against Moldavia the Ottomans withdrew. There was no further fighting until 1484.

The first siege of Rhodes 1480

In 1480 Mehmet the Conqueror turned his attentions against the Knights of Rhodes on their island fortress close to the Anatolian mainland. The Turkish landing was unopposed because the Grand Master d'Aubusson could not spare the manpower from the walls. In command of Mehmet's army was a certain Misac, who began by carefully selecting his artillery positions, because personal experience had taught him the tremendous damage that artillery could do in attack. He targeted points that were both vulnerable and strategic and within days nine towers had been destroyed and the Grand Master's palace had been reduced to ruins.

But a successful besieger of Rhodes also had to take the harbour and the Tower of St Nicholas was the key to achieving that objective. Three hundred balls were loosed at its 24ft-thick walls, which eventually cracked, but fortunately for the garrison the

A Turkish flag captured during the siege of Güns (Koszeg) on display in the castle.

The castle of Buda, taken under direct control by the Ottomans in 1541 after they defeated an Austrian Imperial Army.

rate of fire from the huge siege cannon was not very rapid as the barrels had to cool down, so 14 shots a day was a normal average, and by day and by night the defenders carried out repairs to the walls as quickly as the Turkish cannon could demolish them.

On 1 June the defenders were heartened by the arrival of a supply ship into the commercial harbour. After a ten-day bombardment of St Nicholas Misac launched an amphibious dawn attack on the harbour using triremes that had been stripped of all non-essential equipment. There was no attempt at surprise – the Ottoman Army attacked with its customary din from drums and musical instruments – but as the triremes entered the harbour they came under attack from the section of the harbour walls defended by the Tongue (Division) of France. Soldiers who tried to land in the shallows became caught in defensive stakes, and the attack was driven off with the loss of one ship and half the attackers.

On 7 June Misac began a long and carefully planned operation against the sections of wall dedicated to the Tongues of Provence and Italy. The curtain wall along this length was comparatively thin, so Misac ordered a two-pronged approach of battering the walls and launching balls and incendiary devices over them into the Jewish quarter of the town immediately beyond. The south-eastern wall slowly collapsed into the moat and presented the Turks with an easily scalable ramp.

At dawn the bombardment ceased. There was a brief pause and then a single gunshot ordered the final advance. Great waves of Turks swept across the moat and up the slope that their guns had created, and it was not long before the defenders who had been driven out of the much damaged Tower of Italy saw the Ottoman standard flying from it. Many Turks were beginning to scale the broken wall that led from the Tower of Italy down towards the sea while their comrades provided covering fire from the tower itself. Yet Rhodes still held out, and 3,500 Turks were killed during the repulse of the attack on the breach and the subsequent pursuit. The siege was over, and when Misac finally withdrew his troops after a campaign that had lasted three months, he had suffered a probable casualty list of 9,000 dead and 15,000 wounded.

The Ottoman invasion of Italy 1480

In 1480 Mehmet the Conqueror launched the most audacious expedition of his career when an army under Gedik Ahmet Pasha landed in

The siege of Vienna 1529, as depicted by a print maker who was an eyewitness.

southern Italy and captured Otranto. They then raided inland and struck at Brindisi, Taranto and Lecce, but Duke Ferrante of Naples led a counterattack and drove them back to Otranto. The majority of the Turkish Army then sailed away, leaving a garrison at Otranto who sat there stubbornly during the whole time that Rhodes was being besieged. When Rhodes was abandoned Turkish interest returned to this bold but lonely outpost, which saw fighting well into 1481.

The occupation of Italian lands so close to the main altar of Christendom caused a level of panic that exceeded the reaction to the loss of Constantinople and recriminations were liberally tossed around. The Venetians in particular were accused of doing nothing to prevent the Turkish advance and even of having instigated the invasion. In spite of the retention of Rhodes fear of the Turk was now at its highest. Mehmet the Conqueror himself was said to be coming to Italy and the Pope considered fleeing to Avignon. Instead he asked for help, but it was not the polyglot force he assembled that saved Italy, but the eventual death of Mehmet the Conqueror in 1481.

The heirs of the Conqueror

In spite of all his achievements the work of consolidating the Ottoman gains was not completed when Mehmet the Conqueror died. He left two surviving sons, Bayezid and Jem, each of whom had charge of a province of Anatolia. A clash between them was inevitable. The current Grand Vizier favoured Jem and tried to keep the news of Mehmet's death from Bayezid, but his plot was found out and Jem was defeated. He fled to Rhodes where he took refuge with the Knights. They sent this valuable bargaining counter on to France, and Jem found himself the centre of various crusading plots until his death in 1495.

The result was that Sultan Bayezid II's entire reign was overshadowed by the possibility that Jem might be used as a pretender by the western powers. As long as Jem was alive the Ottomans dared not engage in major wars, so the characteristic activities of Bayezid's reign were raiding and border warfare. Ottoman attacks were made on Croatia and the Austrian lands of Styria, Carniola and Carinthia. In 1493 an Ottoman army was defeated at the battle of Villach.

Peace was restored in 1495 with a three-year truce with Hungary, but the Ottomans still had to win control over the estuaries of the Danube and the Dneister in order to establish safe land communications with the Crimea. So in 1484, Bayezid II concluded an armistice with King Matthias Corvinus of Hungary. This gave him a free hand to attack Stephen the Great of Moldavia. In the same year Bayezid II captured the fortress of Chilia. His campaign into Moldavia was checked by reverses at the battles of Catlaburga in 1485 and Scheia in 1486, but in spite of these defeats Moldavia became an Ottoman dependency.

The capture of Belgrade

Suleiman the Magnificient became Sultan in 1520 at the age of 25. History now remembers him as the greatest sultan of his line, a man who fully justified the two epithets he was given – 'the Magnificent' to Europeans, and 'the Lawgiver' in his native land – but in 1521 his greatness was merely potential. The repression of a revolt in Syria was Suleiman's first campaign. Hungary was the next, and the key to any advance into Hungary was the city of Belgrade, which lies on the southern bank of the Danube at its confluence with the Sava. It had remained out of Ottoman hands in spite of the vigorous siege in 1456 and the capitulation of much of the rest of the Balkans.

The Ottomans had long since been in possession of the line of the lower Danube from Smederevo to the Black Sea, a factor that Suleiman intended to exploit. He left Constantinople for Belgrade on 16 February 1521 and his army was followed up the Danube by a supply convoy of 40 boats. On reaching Nis the force divided. One part, commanded by Ahmed Pasha, the *beylerbey* of Rumelia, moved against Sabac, followed a few days later by Suleiman himself. The second main body under the Grand Vizier Piri Pasha headed for Belgrade, while the *akinji* were also separated into two bodies, the first to act as scouts, the second to raid into the Carpathian mountains of Transylvania.

Sabac defended itself with fruitless heroism, and 100 heads of the soldiers of the garrison who had been unable to escape by river were brought to the Sultan's camp. On 8 July these heads were placed on pikes along his route. Suleiman then proceeded to transfer his army across the river using boats and marched downstream along the northern bank towards Belgrade. Loud cheers from his army, who had already begun a siege from the south, greeted his arrival on the enemy side. An initial assault was repulsed, so Suleiman began bombarding the walls from the island in the middle of the Danube, and 500 *Janissaries* were ordered to go up the Danube in boats to intercept the Hungarians. On 8 August an attack was launched that caused the defenders to abandon the city and retire to the castle, where they held out for a further three weeks. Belgrade only surrendered after one of the main towers had been destroyed by a mine.

The second siege of Rhodes

Although the 1522 attacks on Rhodes were every bit as fierce as 1480 and delivered with the support of guns even bigger than those used then, the siege proved to be a very different affair from what had been expected. In 1522 the siege operations were conducted as much under the ground as above it. Fortunately for the garrison, some prisoners revealed that Suleiman had recruited many miners from his conquered territories. The acquisition of this information allowed the Grand Master time to bring into his service a renowned military engineer called Gabriele Tadini, who was placed in charge of all counter-mining operations.

The walls of the Knights' defences followed the lines of old culverts, affording the possibility that these tremendous walls, although built upon solid rock, were already undermined for most of their length by old tunnels. The Turkish plan was to drive mines under the moat to connect with the ancient passages where sites could be selected for explosives to bring down towers or to collapse walls. The Turkish assault, however, began in a way very similar to that of 1480 with the installation of cannon batteries for what was to prove a sustained and long bombardment.

On 9 September two mines exploded under the sector of Provence but had little effect due to Tadini's countermeasures, while another under the English sector brought only a minor collapse of masonry. The formidable reinforcements built round the gates were hardly touched, an eloquent testimony to the strength of their designs, although the Bastion of St George still shows a vertical crack to this day. Reinforcements and supplies for the Knights continued to arrive in dribs and drabs while the pattern of mining and countermining, assaults on the breaches and bloody hand-to-hand fighting continued. By the beginning of December the new tunnels added to the ancient culverts had created such a honeycomb beneath the walls that it is surprising that they stood up at all and the garrison were running short of supplies.

Three individual meetings were held between Suleiman the Magnificent and Grand Master de L'Isle Adam during which an amicable settlement was negotiated. The personal trust that bound the eventual agreement between the two deadly enemies is quite remarkable. When Suleiman the Magnificent rode into the city through the Gate of St. John he dismissed his guards, saying, 'My safety is guaranteed by the word of a Grand Master of the Hospitallers, which is more sure than all the armies in the world.' Yet the Sultan's generosity had its downside, because the Knights of Rhodes whom he let sail away unharmed were to become the Knights of Malta.

The battle of Mohacs

Suleiman's next European campaign resulted in the greatest victory of his career. On 23 April 1526 he left Constantinople at the head of an army of perhaps 100,000 men and 300 cannon to advance against Hungary: a kingdom that was divided against itself and almost abandoned by its allies. The long march lasted 80 days before contact was established with the enemy. Dreadful weather added to the Turkish difficulties, and torrential rain increased the current of the Danube so much that the fleet of 800 supply vessels had great difficulty keeping up with the army.

Nevertheless strict discipline was maintained. Soldiers were executed for treading down young crops or even letting their horses graze on them and, in spite of his slow progress, Suleiman was able to take heart from two things. The first was the constant arrival of reinforcements to his standard. The second was the exemplary efficiency demonstrated by his Grand Vizier Ibrahim Pasha. When the Sultan arrived in Belgrade he found a bridge already waiting for him, courtesy of Ibrahim Pasha, who was then sent on ahead once again to capture the fortress of Petrovaradin. It lay on the southern bank of the Danube about midway between the Sava and the Drava near present-day Novi Sad. Two mines opened up a breach in the walls, and the citadel fell to the Turks with a loss to the besiegers of only 25 men.

The time it was taking the Ottoman Army to advance should have allowed plenty of opportunity for King Louis II of Hungary to make defensive preparations. It was obvious to Suleiman that the most likely place for their advance to be stopped was the river Drava, the only river barrier that now remained between the Sultan and Hungary since the fall of Belgrade. The Drava joins the Danube just below Osijek in Croatia and for much of its length forms the present-day border with Hungary. On their way there the Turks captured Illok on 8 August, in spite of being delayed again by wet weather, and it was not until 14 August that the Sultan reached the junction of the Danube and the Drava. He was expecting to find a huge Hungarian army sitting on the Drava's northern bank. But there was no enemy in sight.

King Louis II had reached Tolna on 2 August, where his allies began to arrive to join him. But personal rivalries prevented them from cooperating effectively. It was to King Louis' great credit that he appreciated as much as did Suleiman the tremendous strategic importance of the line of the Drava. It was very late in the day for it to be secured, but by 8 August there was still time to reach it from Tolna, so the young king ordered Stefan Bathory to occupy Osijek and defend the Drava. But the majority of the Hungarian nobles who were ordered to march with him refused to move. They would only serve under their king, they declared, not his mere deputy. Bathory tried to set them an example of loyalty, even though a bad attack of gout made it difficult for him to mount his horse. But the plan had to be abandoned, and instead of sending a vanguard to the Drava the whole army marched on to a point almost midway between Tolna and Osijek near the little riverside hamlet of Mohacs. John Szapolyai, one of the king's strongest Hungarian allies as well as one of his greatest rivals, was ordered to go raiding.

Meanwhile Sultan Suleiman had dealt with the undefended line of the Drava in a manner that was militarily effective and profoundly symbolic. He gave orders for a bridge of boats to be thrown across the river, a task his enthusiastic followers completed in five days. When all his army were safely across he burned Osijek and then destroyed the bridge itself. There was to be no turning back.

The battlefield of Mohacs is located south of the present-day town of Mohacs along the road to Croatia, and most of the actual fighting probably took place in an area between four and seven miles away from the town. In 1526 most of the land to the east of the present road, including the section now inside Croatia, was swampy woodland. The heavy rain that had dogged the campaign up to that point had made the conditions much worse than normal, and the little river called the Borza, which eventually empties into the Danube, had disappeared into the morass.

The siege of Buda in 1541.

A combination of woods and ridges shielded the Turkish advance from the eyes of the Hungarians. King Louis II set up his standard at a point just over halfway between Mohacs and the Borza River. The Sultan, who was aware of the potential striking power of the Hungarian knights, arranged his defences in depth. A thin screen of *azaps* (conscripted light horsemen) stood out in front. The Rumelian and Anatolian horse, supported by artillery, constituted the first two major lines under the Grand Vizier Ibrahim Pasha and Behrem Pasha respectively. The third line consisted of the heavy artillery with 15,000 *Janissaries* and *sipahis* on the flanks under the personal command of the Sultan himself. Squadrons of cavalry lay to the rear in support, while far over on the left wing, and much advanced towards the Hungarians, stood a force of *akinji*.

The battle of Mohacs began with a salvo from the Hungarian artillery. Then a tremendous charge of Hungarian knights took place across the firm grassland. The shock of the knights' charge broke the Rumelian and Anatolian horse and advanced towards the third line. They looked as though they were about to make contact with the Sultan himself when suddenly they were brought to a violent halt by the fire from the line of Turkish guns that had been chained together along the edge of a depression. Part of the Hungarian left wing gave way and retired to the marshy ground and when the Ottomans launched their counterattack the main body of the Hungarian knights were driven straight back towards the king's camp. There they found to their dismay that some Turkish light horsemen had already arrived and were slaughtering the camp followers.

Meanwhile the detached Turkish units advanced in two sections, one against the flanks of the mêlée that was now threatening to turn into a full-scale Hungarian retreat, and the other on towards the king's position at the rear. The slaughter was finished by 6pm after only two hours of actual fighting. Of the king's estimated 13,000 foot soldiers only 3,000 got away. King Louis II of Hungary completely disappeared. He had fled from the battlefield, but when his horse tried to climb the steep bank of a small stream it fell and landed on top of him, crushing him to death. His body was only found and identified two months later when the floods of the Danube had subsided. A number of prisoners were taken, but the Sultan had them all beheaded the next day.

John Szapolyai eventually arrived at Mohacs the day after the catastrophe, but hurriedly withdrew when the sight of destruction met his eyes. After three days rest Suleiman the Magnificent continued unopposed to Buda, burning the cathedral city of Fünfkirchen (Pecs) on the way. On entering Buda on 10 September he ordered the place to be spared, but it was burned and looted anyway. Many treasures were carted off to Constantinople while the irregular horse raided throughout Hungary. The widowed Queen Mary fled to the safety of Bratislava and then on to her brother the Archduke Ferdinand of Hapsburg, who ruled Austria from Vienna.

Suleiman had already decided not to annexe Hungary but to make it into a tributary principality like Wallachia, and in this decision he was aided by the ambitions of John Szapolyai, who sent envoys to the Sultan at Buda offering his services. As a result of their discussions John Szapolyai entered Buda as the Turkish representative when the Ottoman Army withdrew.

To the family of the late King Louis II the only claimant for the throne of Hungary was Anne, the sister of the dead king who was married to Archduke Ferdinand. A Diet was called in Bratislava on 26 October and elected Anne and her husband as king and queen of Hungary. But three weeks later on 10 November 1526 the Turkish nominee John Szapolyai was also crowned king of Hungary at Szekesfehervar. So to add to the massacre at Mohacs and the Turkish subjugation, Hungary now had to suffer the problem of rival kings, a native Hungarian who was the puppet of the Ottomans and the Hapsburg Archduke of Austria. Two centuries of war and disunity were to follow.

The momentum that the victory at Mohacs gave to Ottoman expansion entrenched land warfare as the favoured means of extending the empire's boundaries. The close link between military success and political power that existed in Ottoman society also ensured the reputation of Sultan Suleiman. All Europe expected him to return to the Danube in 1527 to continue where he had left off, but the Turkish Empire stretched into distant domains of which few Europeans were aware and these territories were to occupy him for some time to come.

His Balkan governors nonetheless served to demoralise Hungary still further – not that Hungary needed any external pressure to be demoralised, because a civil war between its two monarchs was already performing that task very successfully. That same year King Ferdinand, with the help of Bohemian troops, drove John Szapolyai's armies out of Buda,

Gul Baba, the hero of the 1541 siege of Buda, depicted in a statue next to the mosque dedicated to him in Budapest.

captured Raab (Gyor), Komoron and Gran (Esztergom) along the line of the Danube and also took Szekesfehervar. Szapolyai naturally appealed to the Sultan for support, but help did not come in 1527, nor did it come in 1528. Instead John Szapolyai became a footnote in the next great Turkish advance against Europe in the most ambitious campaign of the great Sultan's reign.

The siege of Vienna

Suleiman the Magnificnt launched his Vienna campaign on 10 May 1529 and reached Osijek on 6 August with an army of

perhaps 120,000 men. On 18 August he met up with King John Szapolyai and, with the pro-Turkish Hungarian king leading the way, the army of invasion proceeded north. Buda capitulated on 8 September, and John Szapolyai gratefully installed himself within the city while the rest of the army continued on along the line of the Danube. To the dismay of the Austrians several of the fortresses they had recently captured from Szapolyai, including Gran (Esztergom), Tata, Komoron and Raab (Gyor), now surrendered and the only place that put up any sort of defence was Bratislava, from where the accompanying Turkish fleet was bombarded as its sailed upriver. On 27 September Suleiman the Magnificent arrived safely at the gates of Vienna.

Ferdinand's garrison was over 16,000 strong, but his men defended medieval walls from which modern artillery bastions and the like were conspicuous only by their absence. The defences of Vienna therefore paled by comparison to somewhere like Rhodes and the wall that surrounded the city was in many places no more than 6ft thick. We know from accounts of the siege that the usual precautions were taken of levelling the houses just inside the walls and building an inner earthen wall from which a counterattack might be launched. Provision was also made for a rapid breaking down of the bridge across the branch of the Danube that acted as the city's north-eastern moat.

In spite of the weak state of the old-fashioned walls, the Turks realised that they would have to deal with an attitude of determined defence equal to that shown at Rhodes seven years earlier. The quality both of troops and of their leadership far surpassed the shambles at Mohacs. The majority of the garrison were professional soldiers fighting under a soldier who had recently distinguished himself at the battle of Pavia. One of his sorties from the walls, designed to disrupt the digging of sap trenches (which it did successfully), also came within a hairsbreadth of capturing Suleiman's illustrious Grand Vizier, Ibrahim Pasha.

Otherwise it was the time-honoured sequence of bombardment and mining, although the former was much reduced because much of the Turkish heavy artillery had been left behind owing to the foul weather and the latter technique was vigorously countered by sheer bravery. Several Turkish mine heads were detected and blown in and, on 6 October, 8,000 men of the city took part in an attack designed to clear the ground behind the Turkish front line where mines were started. Immense damage was done, although congestion on the army's return allowed the rear companies to be badly cut up.

After a number of attacks had been repulsed an Ottoman council of war on 12 October began to consider the possibility of a retreat. Winter was fast approaching, so Suleiman decided that one final effort should be made. His men were spurred on by the promise of a rich reward to the first man to climb over the wall. But even this could not guarantee victory and at midnight on 14 October screams were heard coming from the Turkish camp as their prisoners were massacred ready for a withdrawal.

The Turkish retreat was disastrous. On land the army struggled through early snow and on the Danube the ships came under fire from the cannons of Bratislava. Suleiman's light cavalry ravaged their way home, but it was calculated that the number of Austrian peasants they killed was smaller than the number of Turkish troops lost during the siege. In Buda King John Szapolyai came out to congratulate his suzerain on a great victory, but the contrast to the confident army that had marched north was very noticeable.

The 'Little War' in Hungary

During 1530 the triumphant Archduke Ferdinand took advantage of the Sultan's absence to recapture Gran and other Danube forts. He even attacked King John Szapolyai in Buda, although the resistance offered by its Turkish garrison drove him off. But

Suleiman was back in Hungary in 1532 for a second try at Vienna with an even larger army than he had brought with him in 1529. He crossed the Drava at Osijek, but instead of taking the usual route for Vienna he turned westwards into the narrow strip of Hungarian territory towards the Austrian border that was still in King Ferdinand's possession. After taking a few minor places he laid siege to a castle that was then, as it is today, the last fortress in Hungarian territory.

The town is now called Koszeg, but in 1532 the Austrians called it Güns. It was a tiny place defended by only 700 men, yet it held out against the Turks for almost as long as mighty Vienna. Its commander was one Miklos Jurisics, a Croatian by birth and a captain of great resolution and integrity. His 700 men had been intended for the general muster at Vienna but stayed behind when they realised the Turks' immediate intentions.

They had no cannon, few arquebuses and little powder, but the siege was started in blissful ignorance of these facts by Grand Vizier Ibrahim Pasha. Suleiman the Magnificent came to join him shortly afterwards. The layout of Koszeg's walls made mining a feasible strategy, but even though several mines succeeded in blowing holes in the fortifications, every subsequent assault was beaten off.

Jurisics was then summoned to a parley in the tent of Ibrahim Pasha to receive his proposals for an extraordinary deal. Suleiman the Magnificent, who still did not realise how small was the force that had delayed him for so long, offered to spare the garrison and march away if Jurisics would offer him a nominal surrender. The only Turks who would be allowed to enter the castle would be a token force who would raise the Turkish flag and keep their comrades out before withdrawing for good. Miklos Jurisics was acutely aware of the desperate straits his tiny garrison were in and agreed to this unprecedented proposal. As a result, while the rains of a miserable August continued, the Ottoman Army withdrew.

The other result of the Sultan's second invasion of Austria was a peace treaty concluded with King Ferdinand. Its terms still maintained the right of John Szapolyai to be king of all Hungary, but recognised Ferdinand's possession of that part of the country that enjoyed the status quo. A breathing space was therefore given to all sides and it would be nine years before Suleiman the Magnificent resumed his land war against Hungary and Austria.

Meanwhile the rival kings Ferdinand and John kept up sporadic hostilities against each other. Ferdinand was the first to break the treaty and sent three of his ablest generals, all veterans of the siege of Vienna, to besiege Osijek in 1537. In this they far outreached their lines of communication. A fierce counterattack by Turkish cavalrymen drove them back along the Drava through the November snows and in a series of running fights near Valpovo (Valpo) in Croatia suffered a defeat that produced a casualty list almost as long as Mohacs.

In 1537 Suleiman the Magnificent produced yet another of those dramatic military gestures that caused periodic panic in western Europe. This time he marched a large army to the coast of Albania and landed it in Italy near Otranto, just as Mehmet the Conqueror had done in 1480. Eight thousand irregular horsemen then raided inland, although Otranto and Brindisi held out. This produced as much terror in Italy as the incursion of 1480 had. But when an expected French invasion of Italy from the north did not materialise the Sultan withdrew all his troops and chose instead to besiege Corfu, an action that led to the indecisive naval battle of Prevesa.

When the pro-Turkish King John Szapolyai died in 1540 his heir was but a few weeks old, so Queen Isabella hurried to have him crowned in his cradle as news of a rapid advance on Buda by King Ferdinand began to reach her ears. Sultan Suleiman came to her aid in 1541, helped immeasurably by the incompetence of the elderly Austrian general Rogendorf. Ferdinand's commander already controlled Pest and should have been capable of crossing the Danube to take Buda, but was not. Having destroyed Rogendorf's

stalemated army outside the city Suleiman crossed to Pest and slaughtered the rest of the Austrians stationed there. The Queen was most grateful, but became suspicious when the Sultan asked for the baby king to be brought to his tent. No harm was done to the child, whom Suleiman swore solemnly to protect. The catch was that, in the Sultan's opinion, this protection would be better exercised if the child and his mother were moved to the safety of Transylvania until the infant, now named John Sigismund, came of age. While these delicate negotiations were taking place a Turkish garrison secretly entered Buda castle. Measures were therefore taken for the direct annexation by the Turkish Sultan of those territories that had hitherto been held by his vassal John Szapolyai.

In April 1543 Suleiman returned for a large-scale mopping-up operation to capture the Hungarian towns that had gone over to the Austrians during Ferdinand's last invasion. Gran (Esztergom), Pecs and Szekesfehervar returned once again to the Turkish fold. All that remained of Hapsburg Hungary was now a long, narrow strip of borderland. It looked as though just one mighty push could take the Sultan again to Vienna, but a further peace agreement allowed young John Sigismund Szapolyai to attain the age of 11. He was also recognised as Prince of Transylvania, where some bitter campaigning deprived the Austrians of all the fortresses they had occupied there.

It was only when the Turks returned to Hungarian territory in 1552 that a further reverse awaited them at Erlau (Eger). It lay almost at the north-western extremity of King Ferdinand's scrap of Hungary and provided the second of three instances when small Hungarian fortresses defied Suleiman the Magnificent. In command of Erlau was Istvan (Stephen) Dobo, whose garrison was sustained by large quantities of the local red wine. Someone who saw the wine dripping from the whiskers of the defenders during the siege claimed that they were fortified by bulls' blood, an appellation that has stuck for the Eger vintage to this day. The women of the town played a gallant part by keeping their menfolk supplied with powder, ball and of course flagons of bulls' blood, while emptying cauldrons of boiling water over the Turkish siege ladders. The result was a second humiliation for another overwhelming Turkish Army.

The Great Siege of Malta

When the Knights of St John moved from Rhodes to Malta they did more than merely occupy another island base. With the same foresight and energy with which they had given Rhodes the finest fortifications they could afford, the Knights converted the rocky island into a formidable galley port where Spanish fleets could rest and re-arm.

Although financial resources did not stretch towards fortifying the area where Valletta now stands, Grand Master Jean de La Vallette, after whom the capital would one day be named, had erected a fine star-shaped fort called St Elmo to guard the harbour approaches. For this reason the Turkish Army came ashore on the west coast of the island and directed their first efforts against Fort St Elmo. This initial operation went on for a full month. St Elmo was contested under the

circumstances of a curious reversal in the physical positions of the two armies, because the Turks attacked by land while the Knights reinforced and supplied the place by sea. This convenient arrangement ended when the corsair Dragut arrived and placed guns at a strategic position to cut off any ships crossing the harbour mouth, even by night. The final capture of St Elmo was expensive for the Turks, who lost 8,000 men for the 600 killed among the defeated. Dragut was killed during the attack and Piale, the commander of the fleet, was badly injured by a ricocheting shot.

With Fort St Elmo out of action Mustafa Pasha was able to bring his whole force round to the harbour of Marsa Muscetto immediately to the north of the Grand Harbour. The inner defences of Malta were now subjected to seven weeks of attack in the second phase of the operation, but the system of walls kept any breaches to a minimum, and the discipline and fighting skills of the soldiers held any breaches that were created.

Early in July a new method of attack was tried. Hassan, the Pasha of Algiers, who was the son of the great Khaireddin Barbarossa,

The castle of Erlau (Eger), site of the siege of 1552.

A scene of fierce fighting between Ottoman troops and Titus Zsondi defending a castle for the Hungarians.

led an attack by small boats on the weak points of Malta's seaward defences while a land assault went on. Both attacks failed, the waterborne one disastrously so when it was found that a boom just under the surface of the water had covered the so-called weak points. In desperation the leader of the unit thrust his boats against the rocky point of the spur and some of his men even got a footing, but they were driven out and exterminated when their boats were caught in a crossfire.

This was the only attempt at an assault on Malta by sea. Otherwise the siege was the usual pattern of mining and bombardment to create breaches and desperate struggles for the gaps thus created, but by the end of August the Turks had had enough and the arrival of a reinforcing fleet served only to confirm them in the decision to withdraw. Malta therefore survived to deny the Ottomans the control of the North African coast that they had sought.

The end at Szigetvar

The defeat at Malta marked the beginning of the final year of Suleiman the Magnificent's life. His woes included serious dissension within his own house, largely over the question of who would become the next sultan. The one thing that might satisfy him was victory in battle, so in January 1566 Suleiman the Magnificent went to war for what was to prove the last time. He was 72 years old, and suffered so badly from gout that be had to be carried in a litter, yet his 1566 campaign was the 13th military expedition he had conducted in person.

The new invasion was also his seventh against Hungary and, on 1 May 1566, Suleiman left Constantinople at the head of one of the largest armies he had ever commanded. His weakened state meant that the host proceeded slowly and only reached Belgrade after 49 days' marching. On 27 June he received in audience John Sigismund

The Ottomans approach Fort St Elmo during the siege of Malta 1565.

ASSEDIO,E BATTERIA DIS.ELMO,
A DI 27 MAGGIO 1565.

Szapolyai, to whom he confirmed his promise to make him ruler of all Hungary. From the Belgrade area Suleiman made ready to move to the northern border area, but he had hardly started on his way when news came of the defeat at the castle of Siklos, in southern Hungary, of one of his favourite generals Mohammed of Trikala. One Miklos Zrinyi, who had fought the Turks during the siege of Vienna over 30 years previously, had brought about the reversal.

Zrinyi was based at Szigeth (Szigetvar), another fortress near the Hungarian/Croatian border. Szigetvar was off Suleiman's planned line of advance, and involved marching away from the army the emperor was known to have assembled near Vienna, but nevertheless the angry Sultan gave orders for a diversion to the west and an attack on Szigetvar.

On 5 August 1566 the Ottoman Army took up its positions around Szigetvar for a siege that was to become the equivalent of Malta on dry land, although the combination of rivers, moats and marshes around Szigetvar made Miklos Zrinyi's castle look very much like an island fortress. The water defences

were fed by the Almas River, a tributary of the nearby Drava, and had been cunningly utilised to surround what was an unusual design of castle. Szigetvar fell into three sections, each of which was linked to the other by bridges and causeways. Although it was not built on particularly high ground the inner bailey, which occupied much the same area as the castle site does today, was surprisingly inaccessible, because two other baileys had to be taken and secured before a final assault could be launched.

Ottoman morale was high. At Szigetvar Suleiman was motivated by thoughts of revenge as well as conquest and spurred on his men with readings from the Koran. A spell of dry weather favoured the besiegers by reducing the water level in the moats, and by 19 August both the old and new towns were in their hands. While a fierce counter-battery bombardment went on, with both sides giving as good as they received, the Turks began to throw material into the moat of the inner fortress to create their own causeway across. Suleiman had high hopes of taking the castle in a second attack delivered on the auspicious anniversary of the battle of Mohacs. But still the castle held out, as it did

The attack on Fort St Elmo during the siege of Malta in 1565.

LA PRESA DI S. ELMO, A DI 23. GIUG.º
1565

again on 1 September. However, for the past two weeks Suleiman's engineers had been busy in the very unglamorous task of digging a mine under one of Szigetvar's principal bastions. This was a very hazardous undertaking against a fortress that was surrounded by water fed from a river. They managed to reach beneath the wall without detection and fired the mine on 5 September. The resulting explosion was more than anyone had dared hope for. An enormous hole now existed at the corner of Szigetvar, and flames had spread to the buildings inside.

The fall of the castle was inevitable, but the Ottoman high command hesitated for a moment, for on that very same day Suleiman the Magnificent died in his tent behind the siege lines. No doubt the immense strain of the current campaign had contributed towards this most unwelcome event, but at all costs it had to be kept secret. Only the Sultan's innermost circle knew of his demise, and the courier dispatched from the camp with a message for Selim, Suleiman's successor, may not even have known the content of the message he delivered to distant Asia Minor within a mere eight days.

Miklos Zrinyi certainly did not know of the momentous development. He was now in command of a battered fortress with only three sides left standing. An assault across the breach could come at any moment, so Zrinyi decided to resolve the issue by leading his men in one last suicidal sortie. He had only 600 able-bodied soldiers left and, with Zrinyi at their head, they charged across the bridge into the Turkish host who were preparing for the final advance. Zrinyi died almost instantly when two bullets hit him in the chest, and very few of the 'gallant six hundred' survived their absorption into the hostile Turkish ranks. The Ottoman Army then surged forwards into the remains of Szigetvar to meet a colossal booby trap when the castle's magazine exploded among them.

Szigetvar had fallen and, with admirable presence of mind, the Grand Vizier forged bulletins of victory in the Sultan's name. They announced that their lord regretted that his current state of health unfortunately prevented him from continuing with the hitherto successful campaign. His lifeless corpse was borne back to Constantinople while those officials in the know pretended to keep up communication with him. Turkish sources state that the illusion was maintained for three weeks, and that even the Sultan's personal physician was strangled as a precaution.

The capture of Cyprus

When Suleiman the Magnificent died in 1566 he was succeeded by his son Selim II. He was otherwise known as 'Selim the Sot' because of his addiction to drink. He is said to have openly announced his intentions of conquering the Venetian possession of Cyprus, the greatest achievement of his reign, even before his accession. Popular legend ascribes his enthusiasm to his preference for Cypriot wine over all other varieties.

In 1568 the Ottoman war in Hungary was brought to an end with a peace treaty that left Selim II free to achieve his objective. The invasion force of about 350 ships sailed for Cyprus on 27 June 1570 and landed without opposition on the southern coast of the island on 3 July. The military operations of the Ottoman conquest of Cyprus fall into two distinct episodes. The first was the seven-week-long siege of Nicosia, which lasted from 22 July to 9 September 1570, and this was followed by the much longer siege of Famagusta, which held out for 11 months between 15 September 1570 and 1 August 1571.

Selim's commander Lala Mustafa began the operation against Nicosia with a feint against Famagusta, but his force was surprised by a sortie. The Venetian attack may have been more successful had not one member of the raiding party mistaken a donkey for a Turkish soldier and opened fire too soon, but the demonstration was otherwise very effective and caused several Turkish casualties. Meanwhile the full Turkish Army finished disembarking.

On 30 July Mustafa began the construction of earthworks for artillery emplacements as close to the walls as he dared. This was accomplished in spite of fierce cannon fire from Nicosia's angle bastions. The return fire from laboriously constructed temporary forts did little damage, because most of the 60lb shots simply buried themselves in the soft earth of the turf-covered slopes that formed the upper part of the bastions. From the defenders' point of view the only disadvantage to this remarkable absorbency factor was that any earth that was dislodged tended to fall into the ditch and thus gradually built up a ramp that would make the Turks' assault that much easier when it eventually came.

In order to prepare for this event Mustafa began sapping forward in long zigzags which went through the counterscarp and into the ditch, throwing out earth and making traverses which were stiffened by wood fascines brought up by horses. From the trenches the Turkish arquebusiers, who were regularly relieved by fresh troops, kept up a constant fire so that no defender dared show his head above the parapet.

On 9 September the 45th and largest attack on the walls of Nicosia was delivered. So fierce was the assault that the prepared entrenchments filled up with the corpses of the defenders. The garrison's lack of ammunition finally allowed the Turks entry. As panic spread through Nicosia the northern Kyrenia Gate was opened, and many tried to escape, only to be cut down by the Turks. At about this time the eastern gate was forced open and the Turkish Army began to pour in. Nicosia suffered a massacre, with only boys and women suitable for the slave market escaping a savage death. Spurred on by religious fury the conquerors also killed all the pigs in the city and mixed their bodies with the slain of the garrison. The plunder was the greatest, they said, since the fall of Constantinople.

An advance guard of Turkish cavalry arrived before Cyprus's other strong point of Famagusta on 15 September. Over 200,000

may have been present, and comment was made that so many soldiers were ready for the assault they could have filled the ditch by each throwing one of his shoes into it. Losses in action were steadily replenished by further troops shipped over from the mainland. At Famagusta as many as 145 guns finally joined in the bombardment, including four huge cannon firing shot of up to 200lb in weight.

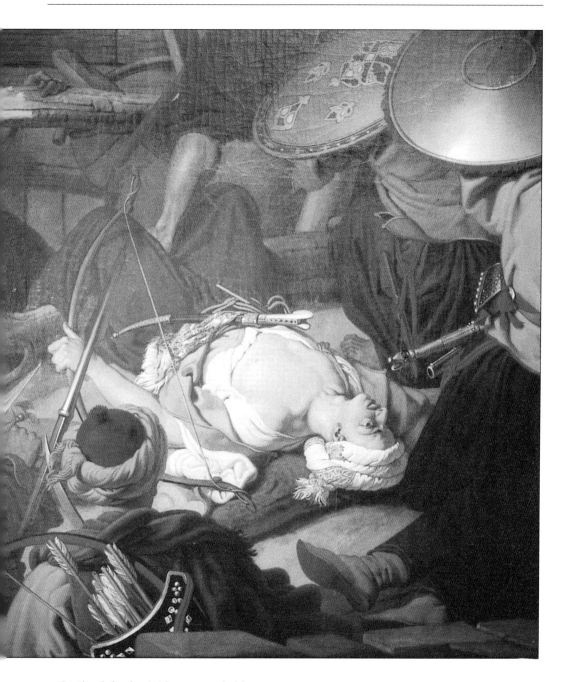

On the defenders' side were probably about 8,500 men with 90 artillery pieces. They were well used and on one occasion a 60lb shot fired over a distance of three miles scattered a review of troops that Lala Mustafa was carrying out in person. The Turks set up an artillery battery on a rocky spur out in the harbour. Other guns from different locations joined in the bombardment and an extensive

A detail from the original painting of the final sally at Szigetvar.

programme of sapping began. Both sides used mines with considerable effect.

The Ottomans then began to lay down an enormous system of trenches using their 40,000 Armenian sappers and local peasants. The result was that for a distance of three miles south of the fortress a maze of zigzagging trenches capable of sheltering the entire Turkish Army covered the landscape, each excavated so deeply that when mounted men rode along them only the tips of their lances were visible. At the point where the saps came within artillery range of the city forts were erected from beams and fascines packed with earth and bales of cotton. In all ten forts were made like this, and the close-range bombardment from them began on 12 May. Heavy arquebus fire also began with an aim of keeping the defenders' heads down, and two hours before dawn on 19 May the fiercest artillery duel of all commenced.

The final Turkish attacks on Famagusta were carried out as a series of hand-to-hand assaults over the heaps of rubble that had once been the city walls. In one incident a Turkish hero called Canbulat charged the Arsenal Tower, where the defenders had apparently rigged up a contraption that spun round a number of sword blades on a wheel.

The final sally out of Szigetvar by Miklos Zrinyi during the siege of 1566.

He was cut to pieces but destroyed the machine and lies buried in the former Arsenal Tower that now bears his name. Few arquebuses were fired to meet the Turks' advance because powder was running so low and an inventory taken on 31 July revealed that only seven barrels of powder of any variety was left. Food was every bit as scarce, so, with still no sign of the relieving fleet, the garrison surrendered on 1 August 1571.

The battle of Lepanto 1571

The famous battle of Lepanto was fought by the Christian fleet that arrived too late to save Cyprus. Instead they located a Turkish fleet at the mouth of the Gulf of Corinth at a place called Lepanto. With such a large navy assembled and with its prime objective lost, it was difficult to resist the opportunity for revenge, so their commander, Don John of Austria, sailed into the attack.

The Christian fleet went into battle in a wide crescent, the main line consisting of galleys ranked close together with a reserve

squadron half a mile to the rear. Don John also had a secret weapon in the form of the galleass – galleys of double the usual size, higher built with overhead protection for their oarsmen and larger and more numerous guns in their bows. Six galleasses fought at Lepanto, and were placed in pairs ahead of the main line of galleys so that their size and firepower would have more impact.

Lepanto was a galley battle in the grand style, because every ship was crammed with soldiers and the tactics used were similar to those of a land battle. The wind was a westerly and blew in the Christians' favour, although they were outnumbered by the Turkish galleys, by 270 ships against 220. As expected, the mighty galleasses broke the Turkish front line, but five or six Turkish galleys immediately surrounded each one. Don John's flagship galley rammed the flagship of the Turkish commander, Ali Mouezinzade, with such violence that the prows of both ships were broken off from the impact, leaving the two vessels stuck together. Don John's troops then boarded the enemy flagship and fierce hand-to-hand fighting took place until Ali Mouezinzade was shot through the head. Someone stuck it on a pike as a trophy.

Similar encounters took place all along the line as individual galleys locked together. It was a scene of utter confusion, but it soon became clear that the Christian soldiers, who were more generously supplied with firearms and better protected with body armour, were gaining the upper hand. Fifteen thousand Christian galley slaves were liberated from their chains, and in the end only six Turkish ships escaped. Their casualties were enormous, running into scores of thousands, while Christian losses totalled 15 galleys sunk and 7,566 dead.

Mustafa Pasha, who had captured Cyprus, returned in triumph to Constantinople to find the capital in a depressed mood because the news of the defeat at Lepanto had preceded him. On the other side the battle of Lepanto was immediately hailed as the salvation of Christendom. In England the people rejoiced with bonfires and sermons,

and the bell-ringers of St Martin-in-the-Fields rang a great peal 'at the overthrow of the Turk'. This was something of an exaggeration. Not only did Lepanto come too late to save Cyprus, it did not cripple the Turkish war effort as much as contemporaries liked to think. So vast were the Sultan's resources that he had rebuilt his fleet by 1573 and time was to justify his boast that on Cyprus he had cut off one of Venice's arms, whereas at Lepanto the Christians had only shorn his beard. Nevertheless, Lepanto broke the spell of the Ottomans' invincibility at sea.

The loss of Cyprus was felt particularly heavily in Venice and in 1573 a new treaty was signed with the Ottoman Empire. This left Spain as the main Christian nation to take on the Turkish Navy and Don John of Austria captured Tunis, only to lose it again in 1574. Spanish attentions were now turning far more to their problems in the Low Countries, but it was not long before the Ottomans were presented with different challenges of their own. In 1578 a 12-year-long war broke out between Turkey and Persia that was to absorb the best of men and materials of the Ottoman Empire, leaving few resources to be diverted back to Europe when a new challenge emerged.

New threats from the north

Turkey's relations with Russia had originated through contacts in the Crimea, and were mainly concerned with commerce and the depredations produced by Tartar and Cossack raiders. But a new challenge arose for the Ottomans from this direction when Ivan the Terrible captured the great Muslim city of Kazan on the Volga in 1552. Two years later King Philip of Spain met a Russian trade delegation while he was in England to marry Mary Tudor. Negotiations began, during which it was agreed that he would supply the Tsar with arms and artillery for use against the Ottomans. No immediate conflict followed, but by 1576 it was clearly recognised in Constantinople that the religious ties between the Russians and the

Suleiman the Magnificent in camp outside Szigetvar.

Ottomans' Orthodox subjects had the potential to cause divisions in the future.

In May of that same year Stefan Bathory of Transylvania was crowned king of Poland. Bathory had dreams of a great central European kingdom from which he could advance to the expulsion of the Turk from Europe. Fortunately for the Ottomans (who had not objected to his promotion even though he was nominally a Turkish vassal) most of his warlike energies were directed against Russia. The death of Stefan Bathory in 1586 restored calm. Two years later tensions were raised again between Turkey and Poland. The election of a new Polish monarch of whom the Ottomans did not approve and a huge raid into Ottoman territory by Cossacks, freed now from Stephen Bathory's restraining hand, nearly caused an invasion of Poland by the Ottomans.

The Thirteen Years War

The conclusion of the Persian war had finally left the Sultan's hands free, but his

European enemies had taken precautions by building new frontier fortresses and restoring old ones such as Kanicsa (modern Nagykanizsa), Raab (Gyor), Komarno (in present-day Slovakia) and Erlau (Eger). These fortresses challenged their Turkish-held equivalents in places such as Gran (Esztergom), Buda, Stuhlweissenburg (Szekesfehervar) and Temesvar (Timisoara in present-day Romania). The Austrians under their rulers from the Hapsburg dynasty also began a policy of settling refugees from Turkish lands along the borders and providing support for these 'marchers', who received land, finance and religious privileges in return for military service.

War between the Ottoman Empire and Austria broke out again in 1593 and once again it was the 'front-line state' of Hungary that saw most of the fighting. In a further echo of the 15th-century situation, the conflict from the European side rapidly assumed the character of a crusade, in spite of all the contempt that the Reformation had heaped upon that long-discredited concept. This Christian optimism was sustained by the persistent belief that once serious warlike moves were made against the Ottomans the peoples of the Balkans would rise up against their occupation.

The Ottomans were also faced with a far more professional force of soldiers than others they had encountered in the past. Defending the Austrian borderlands with Hungary were mercenaries who had fought in the harsh conflict in the Low Countries. They were experienced and well armed, as was shown when a force of Ottoman *ghazis* raiding into Croatia from Bosnia was thoroughly routed at Sissek in 1593. This battle provided what were to become the opening shots of a long war.

Personal and dynastic ambitions also played their part. In 1593, the year the Thirteen Years War began, the three key principalities of Moldavia, Wallachia and Transylvania each acquired new rulers and each opposed the Ottomans. Very soon these princes were in command of the lower Danube, thereby depriving the Ottomans not only of forts and territories but also of the food supplies they were accustomed to draw from the coastal lands of the Black Sea.

The church of St George of the Greeks in Famagusta showing holes caused by cannon fire during the siege of 1571.

An angry Ottoman response soon materialised. On hearing of the defeat at Sissek the Grand Vizier Sinan Pasha threw Emperor Rudolph's ambassador into prison and marched against Hungary with the whole of the Sultan's European levies and 13,000 *Janissaries*. He first captured Veszprem, the Hapsburgs' most outlying fortress, but failed to go any further when the *Janissaries* mutinied against the promise of a winter campaign. Sinan Pasha returned to Hungary the following year (1594) with a

The modern statue of Suleiman the Magnificent at Szigetvar.

much augmented army – perhaps the largest seen since the days of Suleiman the Magnificent. The move obliged the Austrians to abandon a siege of Gran on the south bank of the Danube, opposite the shores of present-day Slovakia, and retire across the great river. With Gran relieved Sinan Pasha could turn his attentions against Raab (Gyor) and he captured this important fortress. He then laid siege to Komarno, but this powerful base across the Danube held out long enough for the approach of winter to force the Ottomans to withdraw. It was nevertheless a satisfactory outcome for the 1594 campaign.

In 1595 the Ottoman Empire acquired a new sultan who began his reign by eliminating 19 brothers. The new ruler was Mehmet III, and he had inherited a very dangerous situation from his father Murad III. This was largely because the defection of the ruler of Transylvania, Sigismund Bathory, to the imperial cause had exposed the Ottoman right flank. Sinan Pasha led a counteroffensive as far as Bucharest but was forced back across the Danube. It was a great change from his largely victorious campaign of 1594 over in the west.

Elated by the news from the east the Imperial forces carried the fight down the Danube from Austria and finally succeeded in capturing the great fortress of Gran, which had been in Turkish hands since 1543. The fall of Gran occurred in August 1595 after a Turkish relieving force was heavily defeated. Then Visegrad, high on a mountain peak beside the Danube, also fell to the Austrians and in a pattern similar to that seen at the time of Mohacs the other northern Hungarian fortresses held by the Ottomans began to collapse like a deck of cards. Soon bands of Christian horsemen could be seen marauding very close to Edirne.

The new situation was so grave for the Ottomans that the Sultan decided to lead the next campaign in person. His counterattack began in the north-eastern corner of Hungary. Mehmet III accordingly took the field and targeted Erlau (Eger), which lay between the Austrians and their new Transylvanian allies. Erlau fell on 12 October 1596, partly because of treachery from the mercenaries in the garrison. It was nevertheless a gain that must have given immense satisfaction to the Turks, because Erlau was the fortress that had held out so well against Suleiman the Magnificent, sustained by its supplies of bulls' blood. But even better was to come.

The battle of Kerestes

An Austrian army had been on its way to relieve Erlau when the castle capitulated. Archduke Maximilian of Austria and Sigismund Bathory of Transylvania were both present with large armies and decided to risk everything in one huge battle with the Ottoman forces. This was the battle of Kerestes (near modern Mezokeretses in eastern Hungary). Not only was their army a large one, it was also most unusual in its composition, being predominately cavalry rather than infantry, with an additional large artillery arm. Among the cavalry were many *reiters*, the mounted wheel-lock pistoleers who were beginning to dominate European cavalry warfare.

A force of Ottoman cavalry tried to prevent the Imperial Army from taking up its position. They were driven off, and when the main body of Turks arrived Mehmet III could see how his enemies had fortified themselves in a field encampment behind a marshy area fed from a tributary of the river Theiss. The Sultan sent forward a detachment of light Tartar horsemen to try the passage of the marsh. They were forced away, so the Ottoman Army drew up in a similar encampment about a mile away.

On 24 October the Turkish attack began, but was driven off with losses on both sides. Two days later another attack was launched. The Sultan was disinclined to lead it and suggested that he should move to the rear, but this was felt to be bad for morale. The Tartar horsemen began an outflanking movement while the Turkish main body crossed the marsh with wings advanced, the European troops on the right and the Asiatic on the left. The *Janissaries* were in the centre along with the Sultan, who rode beneath the banner of the Prophet. Just as at Mohacs, one detachment (under the junior Vizier Cicala) was kept out of sight.

The Imperial Army had made themselves ready for the expected Turkish attack and when the clash came their cavalry charged out to meet it. On the right wing the Asiatic horse were driven back in disarray across the marsh. Some fled as far as Szolnok – 20 miles away. The Austrian Archduke had ordered that the Ottomans were not to be pursued beyond the river, but his orders fell on deaf ears when his commanders on the field

The Danube bend as seen from Gran (Esztergom), the mighty fortress that changed hands several times during the Thirteen Years War.

realised the opportunity that had come their way. As their right wing rolled back the Turks so their centre companies advanced to join them and destroyed a force of *Janissaries* holding out in a ruined church. The Sultan bravely did not flee, but took up a position behind the abandoned camp.

It was then that the position changed dramatically in favour of the Ottomans, because the victorious Imperialists on the right wing abandoned their pursuit of the fleeing Turks for an orgy of plunder within the Sultan's camp. So rich were the pickings that the greedy knights dismounted to ransack the tents more effectively. This was the moment that Cicala's hidden unit had been waiting for. They charged against the totally disordered mob that had once been the pride of the Imperial cavalry. The routed troops bolted back across the marsh, causing utter confusion in the Austrian rear and soon the Archduke had no one left on the field. All their guns were abandoned to the Turks and

thousands were cut down. So serious was the defeat at Kerestes that it was regarded as being akin to Mohacs in the catalogue of Christian disasters against the Turks. Emperor Rudolf of Austria forbade all Christmas festivities that year as a sign of respect.

Had the Ottomans followed up their victory then the war would not have lasted 13 years, but Kerestes was a battle that the Ottomans had very nearly lost and unwise recriminations followed against units of the Ottoman Army whose performance was regarded as less than satisfactory. The Sultan's harsh reprisal measures caused a revolt that nullified many of the gains of Kerestes. A truce was in fact proposed, but as neither side could accept each other's peace terms the war dragged on.

Siegework now became the order of the day and, in spite of the slaughter at Kerestes, the Austrians managed to put two armies into the field by the summer of 1597. No grand Turkish Army advanced to meet them. Instead the responsibility was left in the hands of the Junior Vizier Mohammed Satourdji, who had been left in command of the Danube line. One Imperial army under

The tomb of Canbulat, the Turkish hero of the siege of Famagusta in 1571, who is buried in the tower that now bears his name.

the Archduke Maximilian captured Papa and Totis (Tata), while the Transylvanians besieged Temesvar (Timisoara). In 1598 matters deteriorated even further for the Ottomans when the Austrians recaptured Raab (Gyor) and Veszprem. They even laid siege to Buda and thwarted a Turkish attack under Satourdji on Grosswardien (Oradea in present-day Romania).

The embarrassments of 1598 stung the Ottomans into mounting a more vigorous response in 1599. Their campaign began

with the execution of the unfortunate Satourdji, but the subsequent advance ended with a feeble effort to threaten Gran and the army pulled back to Belgrade for the winter. In 1600 the Turks did much better, recapturing Papa through the treachery of some French mercenaries who sold the fortress to the besiegers. Not daring to move against Gran, the Grand Vizier besieged and captured the supposedly impregnable Kanicsa (modern Nagykanisza). This was an important gain, and the Austrians wasted much time in two unsuccessful efforts to recapture it in 1600 and 1601. But by now the pattern of capture and recapture was becoming depressingly familiar. In 1601 Stuhlweissenburg (Szekesfehervar) was captured by the Austrians from the Turks, but they lost it again in 1602, when there was also a further long and indecisive contest for Buda and Pest.

In 1603 Sultan Mehmet III died and was replaced by his 14-year-old son Ahmed I. War was looming again on the Persian front, so negotiations with the European enemy seemed advisable. There were problems on the Christian side too. Their attempt to prise Transylvania out of the Turkish sphere of influence had been reversed by the disaster of Kerestes. In 1601 the pro-Turkish Stefan Bocksai had been elected prince of Transylvania, and in 1605 he formally allied himself with the Ottomans. His support helped in a final flourish of Turkish success so that in the course of that year the Turks retook mighty Gran, Visegrad and Veszprem. But both sides were now ready for a settlement, and the result was the Peace of Zsitva-Torok, signed in 1606, which brought to an end the bloody Thirteen Years War, described by a Christian commentator as 'the slaughterhouse of men'.

Konstantin Mihailovic, the Serbian *Janissary*

Few *Janissaries* ever had the opportunity, or even the inclination, to return to the Christian fold. Far less ever thought to record their experiences in writing and for this reason the testimony of Konstantin Mihailovic, the so-called Serbian *Janissary*, is of immense interest and importance.

Konstantin Mihailovic was a native of Ostrovica, a town difficult to locate for certain but probably identical to the Ostrovica about 40 miles south of Belgrade. His memoirs tell us nothing about his early life. Instead we are introduced to him at the siege of Constantinople in 1453 where he claims to have been present, although this may be a fabrication. He implies that he was one among 1,500 cavalrymen supplied by George Brankovic, the Despot of Serbia, under the requirements of his vassalage to the Turkish Sultan. Konstantin's narrative is somewhat stilted here. He wants to record his involvement in this major historical event, but is also reluctant to admit that he was required to serve on the Turkish side. As Konstantin was only a boy it is unlikely that he took part in any fighting, and none is recorded in his memoirs. Instead we have some vivid eyewitness descriptions of some of the key moments of the siege such as the dragging of the Turkish ships overland into the Golden Horn.

By the time his story has become more reliable the political problem has disappeared, because the Turks have now invaded his home country and Konstantin is involved in the resistance against them. This was Mehmet the Conqueror's second Serbian campaign of 1455. Starting from Edirne, the Ottoman Army marched via Sofia and laid siege to Novo Brdo, which capitulated on 1 June 1455 after a siege of 40 days. This was the occasion when Konstantin was captured:

the Emperor [i.e. the Sultan] himself standing before the small gate sorted out the boys on one side and the females on the other, and the men along the ditch on one side and the women on the other side. All those among the men who were the most important and distinguished he ordered decapitated.

The boys were taken 'into the *Janissaries*', and Konstantin was among them:

I was also taken in that city with my two brothers, and wherever the Turks to whom we were entrusted drove us in a band, and whenever we came to forests or mountains, there we always thought about killing the Turks and running away by ourselves among the mountains, but our youth did not permit us to do that.

Konstantin's mention of his youth clearly refers to the unlikelihood of them being able to overpower their captors, but flight was still possible:

for I myself with 19 others ran away from them in the night from a village called Samokovo. Then the whole region pursued us, and having caught and bound us, they beat us and tortured us and dragged us behind horses. It is a wonder that our soul remained in us. Then others vouched for us, and my two brothers, that we would not permit this any more, and so they peacefully led us across the sea.

It is from this time that Konstantin is commonly assumed to have become a *Janissary*. However, we see him in action the following year at the siege of Belgrade, which would not have allowed time for the training required. Also he refers to 'the *Janissaries*' in his account in a way that does not imply that he was actually serving in their ranks.

We may therefore assume that Konstantin was attached to the *Janissary* corps in some way. His account of the events of the siege of Belgrade is very interesting. For example:

The highest lord after the Emperor, named Karadiabassa [Karaca Pasha], was standing on a rampart alongside the great cannon observing, and a cannoneer fired from the great cannon into a wall, and the stone, having torn loose from the wall, struck Karadiabassa in the head. He was not alive for long.

The Sultan was then advised to send the *Janissaries* into the attack. Konstantin watched them going in:

and so they stormed until they got into the city. Four hundred and some Janissaries *were listed wounded, but also some, but not many of them, killed. Then, in a short time we saw the* Janissaries *running back out of the city fleeing and the Hungarians running after them and beating them.*

This was the beginning of the rout described above. Konstantin's next campaign in the Sultan's service was against Trebizond (Trabzon), a land he says that is 'mountainous and great, surrounded everywhere by heathens – all Tartars such as the great Khan':

And also rains fell every day so that the road was churned up as high as the horses' bellies everywhere. And so with great effort we arrived at a mountain in the Trebizond area. The road descending from the mountain was ruined and blocked.

This called for desperate measures, and Konstantin tells us how the Sultan was forced to destroy and burn the supply wagons and give the horses away. The baggage was carried forward on camels instead. The excellent discipline of the

Janissaries is illustrated by the amusing incident that followed, because one of the camels carrying treasure slid off the mountain path. The chest it was carrying broke open, disgorging 60,000 gold pieces. The *Janissaries* immediately mounted guard with their swords until the owner of the treasure came along, and when the Sultan arrived on the scene he demanded to know why the whole convoy had come to a grinding halt:

and immediately the Emperor gave the order permitting anyone who could to pick up the gold

The minaret of Erlau (Eger) is all that remains from the period of Ottoman rule that began with the capture of the castle in 1596.

pieces, and the army moved forward. And it was lucky for those who were there at that time, for some did well in that accident. I too happened upon it but late, for the gold pieces were already where they belonged and only black earth remained, for whoever could had grabbed them up with mud and grass, and from each other's hands as necessary.

The next time Konstantin is in action we find him in the Sultan's advance against the notorious impaler lord: Vlad Dracula of Wallachia. Konstantin's vivid account of the war against this larger than life character is very valuable. He confirms Dracula's use of impalement, and adds the gruesome detail that Dracula cut off the noses from his victims and sent them to Hungary, boasting about how many Turks he had killed.

Konstantin was present at the *Janissaries'* attempt to cross the Danube at Nicopolis:

Then the Emperor immediately ordered that they be given 80 large and well-rigged boats and other necessities for shooting: guns, mortars, field pieces and pistols. And when it was already night we boarded the boat and shoved off downstream in that river so that oars and men would not be heard. And we reached the other side some furlongs below where the Voivode's army lay, and there we dug in, having emplaced the cannon and having encircled ourselves with shields and having placed stakes around ourselves so that the cavalry could do nothing to us. Then the boats went to the other side until the Janissaries had all crossed to us.

Konstantin records that 250 *Janissaries* were killed by cannon fire as they disembarked, but the Turkish cannon fire and the sheer weight of numbers eventually drove the Wallachians away. The Sultan must have been very concerned over the possible outcome, because Konstantin tells us that he distributed 30,000 gold pieces among his troops and assured the *Janissaries* that as a result of their service they would be permitted to leave their property to whomsoever they chose after their deaths. Konstantin then describes the Turkish advance to Tirgoviste and Dracula's surprise attack:

we were always on the lookout for them and every night surrounded ourselves with stakes. Despite this we couldn't always protect ourselves, for striking us in the night they beat and killed men, horses and camels and cut down tents so that they killed several thousand Turks and did the Emperor great harm. And other Turks fleeing before them towards the Janissaries, *the* Janissaries *also beat back and killed so as not to be trampled by them.*

Konstantin spares us a description of the 'forest of the impaled'. Perhaps his lowly rank did not permit him to ride so close to the vanguard and the Sultan? In any case the campaign ended soon, and Konstantin's memoirs go on to tell us about his involvement in the Bosnian campaign of 1463, an action that had fateful personal consequences for him.

And so we marched to Bosnia and came to the lands of a Bosnian prince named Kovacevic. Not knowing that the Emperor was on the march they surrendered to the Empeor. Then they cut off his head ... And from there we marched into the King's land and he (the Sultan) first besieged a fortress called Bobovac. Not having cannon with him he had them cast there below the fortress, and he took the fortress by battering it with these guns.

Bobovac was a small castle in eastern Bosnia. The Bosnian King Tomas fled from his capital of Jajce at the approach of the Turkish Army, hoping to reach Croatia. Part of the Ottoman Army went in pursuit of him while the Sultan besieged Jajce. The king eventually surrendered at the fortress of Kljuc:

And Machmutbassa, having heard this, besieged the fortress, and the next day he negotiated with the king [to come] down from the fortress, swearing on books of soap, of which there was earlier discussion, promising that nothing would happen to his neck.

The battle of Kerestes in 1596, an encounter that was almost as great a Turkish victory as the battle of Mohacs.

Ottoman armour dating from the 16th century.
(The Royal Armouries)

The curious comments about swearing on 'books of soap' rather than the Koran is a fabrication inserted by Konstantin to show the deceit of Mahmut Pasha, because King Tomas surrendered and was executed. In reality Mahmut Pasha was sincere in his desire to save the Bosnian king's life but was overruled by the Sultan.

At the end of the Bosnian campaign Konstantin Mihailovic was left with a garrison of *Janissaries* to defend the fortress of Zvecaj. He appears to have had considerable responsibility because he was given half a year's wages for each *Janissary* and had another 30 Turkish soldiers with him. But their resistance was feeble, because Zvecaj was besieged and captured by King Matthias Corvinus of Hungary. Konstantin was among the prisoners taken, and when his identity became known he was repatriated to the Christian side, rich in experience and memories:

And King Matthias, having taken Jajce with a treaty immediately marched back to the Hungarians at Zvecaj, and we also had to surrender; and whatever Turks were at Jajce and Zvecaj, few of them returned to the Turks, for King Matthias wishd to keep them with him. And I thanked the Lord God that I thus got back among the Christians with honour.

With this event he abruptly concludes his personal reminiscences. The rest of his memoirs, including a large introductory section, are observations and reflections on the Ottoman Army and society. The remarkable document ends with the words:

Lord God Almighty, help faithful Christians against the ignoble heathens, to wipe them out. Amen.

Terror and toleration

As in all wars in world history, civilians became caught in the conflicts that attended the growth of the Ottoman Empire, but any assessment of the physical and social damage sustained has to take account of the destructive capacity of warfare in its medieval and early modern context. Because most conflicts could not achieve quick results owing to a lack of overwhelming firepower the wars were prolonged. This meant that the destructiveness was magnified out of proportion to the weaponry that was actually used. Bursa finally fell not because of military developments but because its food supply was dwindling owing to the policy of destroying the agricultural hinterland on which it depended. This took place over a period of years.

Many of the worst cases of suffering happened when the vassal states tried to hit back against the Ottomans. In 1462 Vlad Dracula of Wallachia wrote a letter to King Matthias Corvinus of Hungary describing how he had killed precisely '23,884 Turks and Bulgarians in all, not including those who were burned in their houses and whose heads were not presented for our officials'. The raids are also described in the later German accounts of Vlad Dracula's life. These are often exaggerated, but the description of the Danube campaign cannot be very far from the truth, because he:

ordered that all these men, together with their maidens, should be slaughtered with swords and spears, like cabbage … Dracula had all of Bulgaria burned down, and he impaled all of the people that he captured. There were 25,000 of them, to say nothing of those who perished in the fires.

When the Ottomans advanced on Wallachia Vlad Dracula realised that he could not face the Ottoman Army in open field combat, so he decided to retreat covered by a scorched earth policy, after which he would launch guerrilla raids on the Turks. This inevitably caused great suffering to the population when Vlad burned fields and destroyed villages in his own territory so as to deny supplies to the enemy. Wells were poisoned and lifestock slaughtered. 'Thus', wrote Dukas, 'after having crossed the Danube and advanced for seven days, Mehmet II found no man, nor any significant animal, and nothing to eat or drink.' The Turkish chronicler Tursun Beg described how:

the front ranks of the army reported that there was not a drop of water to quench their thirst. All the carts and animals came to a halt. The heat of the sun was so great that you could cook kebabs on the mail shirts of the ghazis.

Soon the guerrilla raids began, with stragglers being either beheaded or impaled. On the night of 17 June 1462, when the Turks were well on their way to Tirgoviste (Targoviste), Vlad the Impaler launched a daring night attack on the Sultan's camp. Chalkondylas tells us how:

At first there was a lot of terror in the camp because people thought that a new foreign army had come and attacked them. Scared out of their wits by this attack, they considered themselves to be lost as it was being made using torchlight and the sounding of horns to indicate the place to assault.

Thousands may have been slain, but the raid failed in its primary purpose of killing Mehmet the Conqueror himself because his loyal *Janissaries* rallied. The raiders were driven off and disappeared into the darkness. A few days later the Ottoman Army drew near to Tirgoviste. It had been prepared for a siege like any other medieval town, but with one unique addition. As Chalkondylas relates, Mehmet:

saw men impaled. The Emperor's army came across a field with stakes, about two miles long and half a mile wide. And there were large stakes upon which he could see the impaled bodies of men, women and children, about 20,000 of them … There were babies clinging to their mothers on the stakes, and the birds had made nests in their breasts.

The sight of the famous 'forest of the impaled' persuaded Mehmet the Conqueror, a man who was well used to the horrors of war, to pull back from Tirgoviste.

A Turkish archer.

In the absence of such overwhelming horrors many ordinary people joined in the fighting against the Ottoman conquests. Citizens as well as soldiers defended the walls of Constantinople during the siege of 1422. The final Turkish assault was beaten off by fierce hand-to-hand fighting in which all the citizens joined with whatever they had to hand:

With the help of the Virgin Mary they armed themselves with swords and stones and threw themselves against the enemy, and just as smoke scares a swarm of bees they encouraged each other, everyone with the weapons they had to hand, or even just with bare hands while others has swords and staves. They tied ropes to the platters they were eating from and used the lids of barrels as shields.

The repulse of the Ottomans on this occasion was ascribed to the intervention of the Virgin Mary, the protectress of Constantinople, who appeared on the battlements as 'a woman dressed in purple' – a miraculous apparition acknowledged even by the Turks.

A similar example of civilian fervour occurred during the 1456 siege of Belgrade. The passionate orations of the Franciscan friar John Capistrano resulted in a citizen's army of 6,000 men equipped with scythes and cudgels, who made up in enthusiasm what they lacked in military experience. Together with John Hunyadi's 'regulars' Capistrano's 'people's crusaders' (who almost outnumbered the rest of the army) marched to the relief of Belgrade. They were initially alarmed by the multitude of Turkish tents that were pitched outside the walls 'like freshly fallen snow' and the 400 cannon that accompanied the besiegers, so the volunteers held back while Hunyadi's soldiers began the fight. Hunyadi's first task was to break the Turkish blockade of the Danube, which he succeeded in doing on 14 July. Meanwhile, in a worrying echo of Constantinople, Mehmet's artillery bombardment began to breach the walls of

Belgrade in several places. The assault was led by *Janissaries* on 21 July, who were met by fierce resistance and crude incendiary weapons made from tarred wood, blankets saturated in sulphur and even sides of bacon.

While the Turks were burying their dead the following morning some of the more fanatical defenders disobeyed orders and sallied out to fight. When they were attacked in their turn more hastened out to join them, and what had begun as an unplanned skirmish rapidly developed into a full-scale battle. John Capistrano left the safety of the walls to try to recall the men, but as this proved impossible he decided to harness their enthusiasm and led them into further action. This was so successful that John Hunyadi followed him. Soon the Turks were in full retreat. Even the camp of the *Janissaries* was overrun and Mehmet the Conqueror was knocked unconscious. When he recovered his senses he found that he had been evacuated many miles away in a wagon and was so distressed that he contemplated suicide.

The battle of St Gotthard in 1664 on the Raab River in Hungary, a serious setback for the Ottoman Empire.

Ottoman administration

The Ottomans waged war hard, but they governed their conquests with a light hand. The very nature of the territory they inherited made it vital that people looked after themselves. The Ottomans were always interested in effective forms of self-government. 'They pay great respect to the customs of foreign nations,' wrote a commentator, 'even to the detriment of their religious scruples.' However, there was a great deal of common sense behind the idea. When they acquired the mines of the Balkans they reissued the exemplary Saxon mining laws rather than imposing a new scheme of their own.

The earliest Ottoman warriors were lent strength by the ferocity of their commitment to Islam and showed extreme tenacity and perseverance, characteristics that were undoubtedly linked to their religious beliefs. As for the impact of Islam on the vassal states, the Christians under Muslim rule seem to have enjoyed a greater toleration than was shown to the Orthodox under Latin domination, so resistance was

The fortress of Kljuc, where Konstantin witnessed the surrender of the Bosnian king.

not always as fierce as may have been assumed. Churches might be turned into mosques, while those left in Christian hands suffered certain restrictions such at the prohibition of bell ringing and public processions, but matters could have been much worse. The Orthodox world had the tragic memory of the Fourth Crusade of 1204 to remind them of how well off they were under Ottoman rule by comparison with a western conquest. 'Better the Sultan's turban than the bishop's mitre' wrote one Byzantine scholar. It is also interesting to note that in the case of the inhabitants of the borderlands around the Danube temporary flight and depopulation naturally occurred when war threatened. But when the heaviest fighting was over the peasants returned as rapidly as possible to their lands

Social relationships between the Ottomans and their Christian subjects varied considerably throughout the period covered in this book. The Ottomans' first victims soon learned that the only way to avoid the onslaughts of the *ghazis* was to become subjects of the Islamic state. Non-Muslims could then live under Islam's protection. Many took this path, renounced the ineffective protection provided by the Christian states and sought the refuge provided by subjection. As the Muslim conquerors were careful to abide by these rules this helped greatly in the growth of the Ottoman Empire. Christians and Jews were expected to have their own laws. Everyone was organised in the so-called '*millets*', communities based on faith, and as long as the *millet* did not come into conflict with Islamic organisation and society, paid its taxes and kept the peace, its leaders were largely left to run their own affairs. Contrary to popular belief, 16th-century registers suggest that during that century only about 300 families a year converted to Islam. The empire wanted peaceful tax-paying subjects, not Muslims and certainly not rebels. Trade was the one area of civil life where the Ottomans felt obliged to interfere to maintain the efficiency of their armies and the security of their city streets.

The experience of Ragusa (modern Dubrovnik) is a good illustration of the accommodating method operating on both sides. Its citizens had petitioned the Pope for permission to trade with infidels right after the Turks' first serious victory in Europe. By the 15th century the Ottomans had turned Ragusa into their own Venice, to every successive doge's fury and despair! The Ragusans' behaviour was so mild and noble that by 1347 they had erected an old people's home. By the mid-15th century they had abolished slave trading, forbidden torture, organised a dole, a public health service, a town planning institute and several schools. Perhaps once every 25

years, when their courts were obliged to pass a death sentence on an offender, they had to import a Turkish executioner and the whole city mourned.

Less compliant Ottoman vassal rulers were subjected to a number of requirements. They were forced to send their sons to the Ottoman court as hostages, had to pay tribute and to take part in the Ottoman wars either in person or represented by their sons. Control over their compliance was exercised by the watchful *beys* of the marches. Should any vassal renounce his allegiance, his territory was immediately regarded as a field of battle that would attract the rapid attention of *akinji* raiders.

The Sultan's position

The ordinary subjects of the Ottoman Empire were never under any doubt that they were being ruled by a great dynasty. Mehmet II was the first to take on a quasi-imperial role over his territories. The conquest of Constantinople turned him overnight into the most celebrated Sultan in the Muslim world. Receiving soon the epithet of 'the Conqueror' Mehmet began to see himself as the heir to a world empire. As ruler of the Ottomans his power was in any case unquestioned, but the taking of Constantinople made his world look suddenly much wider. It was a situation summed up ten years later when he was addressed by a Greek diplomat with the words:

No one doubts that you are Emperor of the Romans. Whoever is legally master of the capital of the Empire is the Emperor, and Constantinople is the capital of the Roman Empire.

There was also a third strand in Mehmet's concept of himself as a world leader that derived from the Ottomans' ancient origins in the steppe lands of central Asia. As well as being *ghazi* and Caesar, Mehmet the Conqueror was also the Great Khan.

FOLLOWING SPREAD The second battle of Chocim 1673.

Grand Vizier Mehmet Koprulu

As became its origins in a frontier organisation, the entire Ottoman State was built primarily for war against the infidel. For many years the Sultan led his army into battle in person, a factor that caused enormous strategic problems when the Empire faced war on two or more fronts. Second in command was usually the Grand Vizier, like Ibrahim Pasha at Mohacs. Unique among men of this rank Ibrahim Pasha had been granted a standard of six horsetails, only one less than the Sultan himself.

As the Sultan retreated into obscurity in the early 17th century many more burdens of state gradually passed to the Grand Vizier. As long as he enjoyed the Sultan's confidence a Grand Vizier had enormous power limited only by the world of intrigue and opposition from the *Janissaries*. These factors provided such stress and pressure that only the strongest personalities could hold on to the position for long. Between 1683 and 1702 there were no less than 12 Grand Viziers – a sad decline from the times of the man described here who saved the Empire from itself – but at a terrible cost.

The rise of the Koprulus

In 1654–56 Venice mounted her supreme challenge to the Ottomans at sea in an operation that culminated in a great sea battle in the Dardanelles in 1656. The victory was hailed as a second Lepanto and was followed up by the capture of the island of Tenedos at the mouth of the Dardanelles. In Constantinople the political repercussions of the defeat removed power from the boy Sultan and his powerful mother and placed it in the hands of an elderly but highly capable minister called Mehmet Koprulu.

Mehmet Koprulu Pasha had begun his career as a kitchen boy and had risen steadily in court circles. His innate abilities ensured that he performed well in various roles in the palace, the treasury, on the staff of a former Grand Vizier and as the governor of several provinces. He had been out of office since 1655 and became Grand Vizier in spite of a lack of the formal qualifications. It is said that he accepted the post only on condition that his power should be absolute and unchallenged. All reports presented to the court should pass through his hands.

Law and order were restored with the help of widespread executions and, during the five years he had left to live, Ottoman fortunes revived. On his appointment Koprulu carried out a purge of government officials, an act for which he was uniquely placed. Those notorious for their irregularities were dismissed, among them great dignitaries such as the Chief Treasurer, the Grand Mufti and the commander of the navy. The Chief Eunuch was exiled to Egypt. The commander of the *Janissaries* was executed, as was the Orthodox Patriarch. Altogether the number of victims is said to have exceeded 50,000.

It soon became clear that he desired to restore Turkish fortunes in east central Europe and offered Venice a deal to end the Cretan war. It was turned down, so Koprulu took Tenedos and Lemnos by force. In 1658 Koprulu launched a series of military expeditions that placed obedient puppets on the thrones of Transylvania, Wallachia and Moldavia. Rebellions against the government were also put down with great severity. Among these was the revolt of Abaza Hasan Pasha in 1657/58. A large force was dispatched against the rebels that succeeded in crushing the revolt after heavy fighting.

The Sultan and his mother owed a great debt to Koprulu. He had relieved them of the burden of governing so Mehmet IV could devote himself to the pleasures of the hunt. At hunting parties arranged for him in the Balkans as many as 10,000 of his Christian subjects were taken off their normal duties to serve as beaters and helpers.

In the field of foreign policy Mehmet Koprulu's role was more that of a general. As noted above, having sent the Turkish against the Venetians in the Dardanelles, which broke the Venetian blockade, Koprulu took charge personally of the recapture of Tenedos and Lemnos. He then ordered two large castles, Seddulbahr and Kumkale, to be built to protect the straits against future attacks. Even more important from Koprulu's point of view was the struggle over Hungary and Transylvania. During the years of crisis at the beginning of the reign of Mehmet IV Prince Gyorgy Rakoczi II had attempted to liberate his country from Turkish rule. Koprulu

stepped in and arranged the election of Ference Redei, but two months later Rakoczi expelled him from Transylvania.

Koprulu prepared to lead an expedition in person. He first imposed strict discipline on the *Janissaries* in Constantinople so that they would not take advantage of his absence, and many whom he distrusted were executed. The campaign, backed up by Crimean Tartars and Cossacks, was a huge success and Rakoczi fled to Hapsburg territory.

Korpulu did not live to see the completion of his work in Transylvania. In October 1661 he died at more than 75 years old. His achievements indicated that the Ottoman Empire was capable of surviving if competent men were employed in offices of state, but a regime of terror had been needed before such a situation was brought about. In the eyes of his contemporaries Mehmet Koprulu was not a great statesman but an 'atrocious and ruthless man', but that was what the Empire needed in 1656.

Osman II to Murad IV 1617–48

The war with Poland

Until the beginning of the 17th century the Ottomans had been largely fortunate with their sultans. But with the accession of Ahmed I the quality of their leadership showed an alarming decline. He died in 1617 at the age of 28 and, as his son Osman was then a minor, his pious but incompetent brother Mustafa succeeded him. Only a few months sufficed to show Mustafa's lack of ability to rule, and the boy Osman, then only 14, ascended to the throne in 1618. Young Osman displayed an early thirst for military glory. Not only did

he bear the illustrious name of the founder of the Ottoman line, he also had a strong desire to emulate his great ancestor Suleiman the Magnificent, whose armour he delighted to wear. Thus it was that in 1620 Sultan Osman led the Ottoman Empire to war against Poland.

The basis for discontent between the two countries was the old problem of Cossack raids into Ottoman territories. The Cossacks consisted of former serfs who had fled to freedom and of the urban poor who had

A skirmish between Turks and Hungarians as shown in a statue group in Eger.

The expansion of the Ottoman Empire after the death of Mehmet the Conqueror from 1481 to 1683

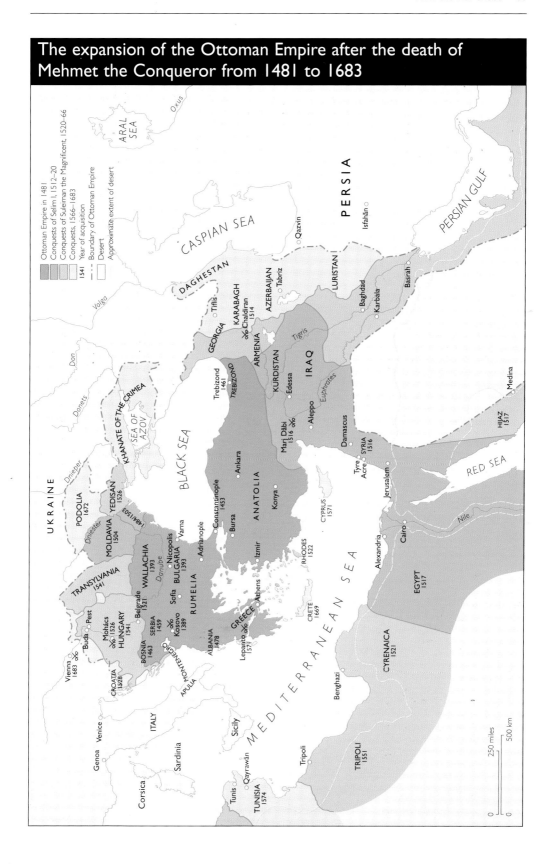

Ottoman Empire in 1481
Conquests of Selim I, 1512–20
Conquests of Suleiman the Magnificent, 1520–66
Conquests, 1566–1683
1541 Year of acquisition
Boundary of Ottoman Empire
Desert
Approximate extent of desert

ARAL SEA

Oxus

PERSIA

Isfahán

PERSIAN GULF

CASPIAN SEA

Qazvin

DAGHESTAN

Volga

LURISTAN

AZERBAIJAN
Tabriz

KARABAGH

Tiflis

GEORGIA
Chaldiran 1514

ARMENIA

KURDISTAN

Baghdad

Karbala

Basrah

Tigris

IRAQ

Euphrates

Edessa

Don

Donets

KHANATE OF THE CRIMEA

SEA OF AZOV

Trebizond 1461
TREBIZOND

Aleppo

Marj Dābiq 1516

Medina

HIJAZ 1517

BLACK SEA

Damascus

SYRIA 1516

RED SEA

Tyre
Acre

Jerusalem

Nile

Dnieper

UKRAINE

PODOLIA 1672

Dniester

MOLDAVIA 1504

YEDISAN 1526

1481/1503

Constantinople 1453

Ankara

ANATOLIA

Konya

CYPRUS 1571

Varna

Bursa

Izmir

RHODES 1522

Alexandria

Cairo

EGYPT 1517

TRANSYLVANIA 1541

Nicopolis 1393

WALLACHIA 1521

Danube

BULGARIA 1393

Adrianople

Sofia

RUMELIA

Athens

GREECE

CRETE 1669

Belgrade

SERBIA 1459

Kosovo 1389

Mohács 1526

HUNGARY 1541

Buda
Pest

Vienna 1683

CROATIA 1528

BOSNIA 1463

MONTENEGRO

ALBANIA 1478

Lepanto 1571

APULIA

ITALY

Genoa
Venice

Corsica

Sardinia

Sicily

Tunis
Qayrawān

TUNISIA 1574

Tripoli

TRIPOLI 1551

MEDITERRANEAN SEA

Benghazi

CYRENAICA 1521

250 miles

500 km

settled in the plain along the Dneiper River. They acted as a military brotherhood, and more than one king of Poland had found them very useful for defending the extreme edges of his domains. They raided Turkish galleys and invaded Ottoman dominions along the Black Sea coast.

The pretext for war in 1620 was more immediate and came about as a result of the activities of Bethlen Gabor, Prince of Transylvania and vassal of the Ottoman Empire. Like so many of his predecessors the Transylvanian ruler proved to be the loose cannon of Ottoman politics, and in 1618 Gabor had taken the part of the Bohemian rebels in the conflict that was destined to become the Thirty Years War. Bethlen Gabor's intervention took the dramatic form of a siege of Vienna and following an agreement dating back to 1613, the Polish king, Sigismund III, was obliged to aid his brother-in-law, the Emperor, against Gabor's Protestant threat. The Polish Diet, however, refused to sanction such an operation, so Sigismund hired out of his own purse a motley crew of mercenaries, adventurers and Cossacks and defeated Gabor in 1619.

Much hurt, Bethlen Gabor intrigued with his master, the young Sultan Osman II, to provide a suitably united Ottoman response. The opportunity came in 1620 when an Ottoman army invaded Moldavia to depose its ruler, Gratiani, who was friendly to Poland. Gratiani appealed to Poland for assistance, assuring the Poles that he would supply 25,000 men. The Polish Army under the Hetman Zolkiewski was a much smaller force. Only 8,000 men advanced to Moldavia where a mere 600 Moldavians joined them. This was instead of the promised 25,000 because the Cossacks had refused to join in.

Heavily outnumbered, Zolkiewski pitched camp at Cecora on the Prut River where he successfully withstood repeated attacks from the Turkish Army under Iskander Pasha. After 11 days Zolkiewski ordered a retreat. For eight days the Poles conducted a fighting withdrawal, but discipline broke down and the Ottomans attacked again. This time the assault was successful. The severed head of the veteran Hetman Zolkiewski was sent to the Sultan as a trophy of war, and his colleague the Hetman Koniecpolski was captured.

The disaster at Cecora aroused all of Poland, and the Diet made provision for the recruitment of 40,000 Cossacks. Within a year a newly formed Polish army was on the march. They assembled near Lwow, and marched to the Ukraine. News was brought to the Polish commander the Hetman Chodkiewicz that a huge Ottoman army was on the move, so the Poles and Cossacks fortified themselves inside their camp at Chocim on the Dniester River. They were soon surrounded by a Turkish army of three times the size under the personal command of Sultan Osman II.

For five weeks the Ottomans assaulted the camp, and when the Poles counterattacked with their famous winged hussars the Sultan negotiated a settlement. It was an honourable agreement by which Poland swore to restrain the Cossacks and the Turks likewise restrained the Tartars from invading Polish lands. The Poles returned well satisfied after a victory that was to provide them with heroic ballads for many years to come, but Sultan Osman's return to Constantinople was an ignominious one. The *Janissaries* were now the power behind the throne, and a defeated sultan had little chance of controlling them. A helpful adviser suggested that Osman should go into Asia and recruit a new army with which he might defeat the *Janissaries*. It was even mooted that the Ottoman capital should be moved east.

Rumours of the plot leaked out and stirred the *Janissaries* to revolt. In May 1622 Osman was deposed and shortly afterwards strangled. The ex-Sultan Mustafa, his mind further weakened by four years of confinement, was dragged back to the throne. With a pliant sultan in charge the *Janissaries* could increase their demands, and their excesses almost bankrupted the state. Yet Mustafa was so hopeless that the *Janissaries* began to regret having got rid of Osman, so his executioner was put to death and Mustafa was replaced once again. The new sultan was one of his younger brothers, then aged 12. The accession of Murad IV took place so quietly that the English ambassador commented that 'emperors are made here with less noise than a proctor at Oxford'.

The year of Murad IV's accession saw the renewal of the war with Persia, which lasted intermittently until 1639. As a result the convulsion in Europe caused by the Thirty Years War was carried on with little likelihood of any serious intervention from Turkey. The notion of a crusade against the Ottoman Empire was occasionally revived, usually because of the presence in a European court of some pretender to the Ottoman throne. But there was little prospect of success for any enterprise arising out of such intrigues and the archaic schemes caused little lost sleep in the Topkapi Palace.

Throughout this time Murad IV's domestic position gradually improved, until by 1632 he began to exert a firm rule and set in motion a series of necessary reforms. His invigorated army finally triumphed over Persia, but scarcely a year after his triumph Murad IV died in 1640. He was succeeded by his brother Ibrahim, under whose reign the Ottoman Empire undertook a new and aggressive war against Europe.

The trigger for renewed fighting with the Ottoman Empire came from the activities of the old knightly orders, in particular the Knights of Malta. Relying on the cloak of pious immortality bestowed upon them for their victory in 1565, the knights played the pirate as much as any Barbary corsair. They preyed on friend and foe alike and their activities did more than anything else to poison the relationship between the Turks and Europe. One commentator expressed the opinion that their activities had 'kept on the alert a monster who might otherwise have sunk into slumber'.

Venice actively discouraged her subjects from having anything to do with the Knights of Malta, but found it impossible to close her harbours to the Maltese galleys. One of the most important of these harbours lay on the island of Crete. In 1644 a Maltese squadron encountered a number of Ottoman vessels laden with a rich cargo off Rhodes. The knights captured the ships and headed for Crete. The incident strengthened the arm of factions in the Ottoman court who were hostile to Venice. The winter of 1644/45 saw the Ottomans engaged in preparations for war against the Venetian territory of Crete in a manner very reminiscent of the preliminaries to the assault on Venetian Cyprus in 1570.

On 30 April 1645 the Ottoman fleet sailed via Chios and Navarino. They landed troops on Crete and took Canea. They had committed themselves to a long and arduous war that was to last 24 years. At first the operation favoured the Turks. The rule of Venice in Crete was as oppressive against the local population as it had been in Cyprus and, although there was no prospect of a mass rising of the people in the Ottomans' favour, certain strongpoints had fallen to the Turks by the end of 1646. In the summer of 1647 the Turkish commander began a blockade of Candia (Heraklion) and commenced a siege against its fortifications in April 1648.

The Venetians regarded Candia as the lynchpin of their entire operations. As long as Candia held out Crete could not become Ottoman and Venetian ships could operate elsewhere in support. The offensive operations by Venice were largely carried out at sea and a major plank of their strategy was to try to cut off the Dardanelles to halt the flow of supplies to the besieging Turkish army. To counter the Ottoman threat they improved the fortifications in the Dardanelles. Unfortunately for Venice the sea route via Chios allowed another exit from Anatolia and Venice did not have the resources to maintain two blockades at once in spite of the regular support provided by the Knights of Malta.

In 1647 Sultan Ibrahim was deposed and replaced by his seven-year-old son Mehmet IV. During his long minority administrative inefficiency and a struggle for power at court led to a very ineffective prosecution of the war with Venice, but not its abandonment. A further boost was given to the western powers by the signing of the Treaty of

The great siege of Vienna in 1683.

The Ottoman Eastern European front during the 17th century to the Treaty of Karlowitz in 1699

Westphalia in 1648. The Thirty Years War was at an end, and they could now concentrate on the threat from the east.

The life and achievements of Mehmet Koprulu, described in detail above, dominated the period that followed. Mehmet Koprulu was succeeded as Grand Vizier by his son Ahmed in 1661. He ruled until 1676 and celebrated the newly invigorated Ottoman power by launching a war against Hungary in 1663. It began as a raid on a grand scale, but when they returned the following year it was to find that the Imperial Army had been improved and enlarged. Resistance was now under the command of a brilliant Italian general called Raimondo Montecuccoli, who had reinforced the key position of Raab. Ahmed arrived in strength before the fortress of Komarom and there was the strong prospect of a peaceful agreement being reached, but he decided to force the issue. While the text of the treaty was still being discussed he advanced up the left bank of the Raab River. Here he met Montecuccoli's army at St Gotthard. The Turks attacked on 1 August with superior forces, but had made the mistake of not bringing all their troops across the Raab. They lost about 5,000 men and 15 guns in a crushing defeat. The battle of St Gotthard indicated the Austrians' growing superiority in land warfare.

The reversal on land encouraged Ahmed Koprulu to pursue the long war for Crete instead and in 1669 Candia surrendered and the Venetians abandoned the island. This success freed Turkish forces for other possibilities and the Ukraine once again became a hotbed of conflict. The native Cossacks sought Turkish help as they attempted to win independence from Russia and Poland. In 1672 a large Turkish army

Nach dem der Türck belegert hat
In Osterreich die Wiener stadt
Da sint auch sein hußern arck
Gestreiffet vierzig taufent starck
hinein das Lendlein ob der Ens
Durch alle flecken darnach sens
Biß yn die Steyer marck gestraifft
Die gätze ländtschafft gar durch schweyfft
Die Flecken verheert vnd verprendt
Frawen vnd Junckfrawen geschendt
Der Cörper man findt auff der straß

Viel hingefürth sölcher maal
Kein grawsamkeit habens vermidten
Kinder aus müter leib geschnitten
Die felben an yhr spies gestecket
O Christen mensch sey auffgewecket
Wirstu von fünden nit absteen
So wirdt es dir gleich also gen
Gestrafft wirdt dein vndanckparkeit
Die Art ist an den Baum geleith ꝛc.

b S S

1 5 3 o.

Turks with captives, the fate of the Serbian *Janissary* Konstantin Mihailovic.

marched into Poland, conquered the fortress of Kamenec (Kamieniec Podolski) and advanced as far as Lwow. They were not to know it at the time, but this operation meant that the Ottoman Empire had attained the largest dimensions in Europe that it would ever enjoy.

The Poles hit back and King Jan Sobieski achieved a victory at the second battle of

Chocim in 1673. But honours were so even that Ahmed Koprulu was able to crown his career by dictating the terms of the Treaty of Zuravno to John Sobieski in 1676. Much of the Ukraine passed into Ottoman hands. It was Ahmed's last gain for his empire. A fortnight later he was dead.

The siege of Vienna

Ahmed Koprulu was succeeded as Grand Vizier by his brother Kara Mustafa, who abandoned Ottoman efforts in the Ukraine for a renewed move against Imperial Austria. He spent several years building up his army and in 1683 moved into the attack for the campaign that is probably the best known of all the Ottoman/European encounters: the siege of Vienna.

The number of Kara Mustafa's army is not known exactly. It may be that the original plan was to capture Raab (Gyor) and Komarom, not Vienna, and none of the initial movements suggested that the capital was threatened. The Ottoman Army advanced up the Danube and crossed the Raab, where a small force was left behind as a pretext of besieging Raab. After a week's march the Turks reached Vienna and began to besiege it.

One hundred and fifty-four years had passed since the first siege of Vienna in 1529. The Turks had possessed no heavy guns then and it is strange to note that they also had none in 1683. Mining was tried, but the garrison replied with spirited counterattacks, and all the while a relieving army was gathering. But by the time it arrived the fall of the city was imminent. The allied army signalled their arrival to the desperate citizens and fell on the Ottoman Army. Led by King Jan Sobieski and his winged hussars the Turks were driven from the field. It was the beginning of a long retreat for the Ottoman Empire.

The Ottoman decline 1683–99

Following the defeat at Vienna the Hapsburg commanders were quick to exploit the situation. As early as mid-October they captured Gran and, after his return in disgrace, Grand Vizier Kara Mustafa was strangled. In 1686 Prince Eugene of Savoy stormed Buda, a victory that sent much of Europe into raptures. English volunteers, including the son of Prince Rupert, fought in Eugene's Army.

There was an Ottoman attempt to fight back. In 1687 a restored Turkish army gave battle at Mohacs – the same site as the epic victory of 1526. But this time the honours went to the Christian side, who followed up their success by invading Moldavia,

Prince Eugene of Savoy at the fall of Buda in 1686.

Wallachia and Croatia. Meanwhile the Venetians attacked in south-east Europe, invading the Morea, capturing Athens and Corinth. The former victory had the tragic result of destroying the Parthenon, which the Turks were using as a powder magazine. In 1688 Belgrade fell and then Nis.

It was only the withdrawal of Austrian troops to meet the threat from France that gave the Ottomans a breathing space. Constantinople had seen repeated changes of Sultan, for neither Suleiman II nor Ahmed II lasted long. A Turkish counterattack recaptured Belgrade and Nis, but this was mere delay and in 1697 Sultan Mustafa II insisted on leading the army in person for the recovery of Hungary. Prince Eugene of Savoy followed their moves and at first

expected an attack on Peterwardein (Petrovaradin), but was required to set in motion a forced march that caught the Turks when their army was half across the river Tisza near Zenta. Here he defeated the Ottomans at the decisive battle of Zenta, 'a frightful blood bath' in Eugene's own words, helped by a mutiny of the *Janissaries,* who killed the Grand Vizier in their desperation. Eugene followed up his victory by a march as far as Sarajevo, but his army was tired and the peace talks that soon got under way cannot have been unwelcome to them. By the treaty signed at Karlowitz in 1699 the Turks conceded most of Hungary, including Transylvania, to Austria, returned Podolia to Poland, confirmed the right of Russia to occupy the port of Azov and made over most of Dalmatia, Morea and the Aegean islands to Venice. The Ottoman Empire was defeated and humiliated.

The Treaty of Karlowitz marked a final and decisive turning point in the military balance between the Ottoman Empire and Europe. It was the first agreement signed between the Ottoman Empire and a coalition of western powers and the first ever formal acknowledgement of an Ottoman defeat. After Karlowitz the Ottomans found themselves permanently on the defensive and rarely able to equal the armed strength of any European power. Internal disorders and the activity of Balkan brigands, a trend that was later to merge with nationalist resistance movements, contributed to the military weakness. From 1716 onwards Ottoman officials made sporadic efforts to recreate Turkish armies on the European model, but for more than a century the conservatism of the *Janissaries* brought most efforts to nothing. Karlowitz had been a real turning point, and for Europe the fear of the Turk had finally passed away.

Glossary

akinji	raiders, the successors of the *ghazis*
askeri	military, infantry auxiliaries
azaps	conscripted light horsemen
beglerbeg	see beylerbeyi
bey	leader
belerbeyi	provincial governor general appointed by the sultan
beylik	principality
cebeci	armourer
deli	maniac, used for shock trooper
emir	commander
ghaza	holy war
ghazi	holy warrior or territory acquired by a holy war
Janissary	elite of the Ottoman Army
jihad	Holy War
millet	non-Muslim citizen, or their quarter
sanjak	province
sanjak bey	leader of *akinji*
sipahi	horseman, feudal cavalry
timar	fied or stipend
topcu	gunner
vezir	Turkish spelling of vizier, minister of state
yamak	auxiliary

Further reading

Coles, P., *The Ottoman impact on Europe* (Thames and Hudson, 1968)

Goodwin, Godfrey, *The Janissaries* (Saqi Books, London, 1994)

Goodwin, Jason, *Lords of the Horizons – A History of the Ottoman Empire* (Chatto and Windus, 1998)

Hegyi, Klara, and Zimanyi, Vera, *The Ottoman Empire in Europe* (Corvina, Budapest, 1986)

Inalcik, Halil, *The Middle East and the Balkans under the Ottoman Empire: Essays in Economy and Society* (Indiana University Turkish Studies and Turkish Ministry of Culture, Joint Series Volume 9, 1993)

Kafadar, Kemal, *Between Two Worlds – The Construction of the Ottoman State* (University of California Press, 1995)

McCarthy, J., *The Ottoman Turks: An introductory history to 1923* (Longman, 1997)

Mihailovic, K., *Memoirs of a Janissary*, translated by Benjamin Stolz (University of Michigan, 1975)

Murphy R., *Ottoman Warfare 1500–1700* (UCL Press, London, 1998)

Nicolle, D., *Armies of the Ottoman Turks 1300–1774* (Osprey Men-at-Arms 140, Osprey Publishing Ltd., Oxford, 1983)

Oman, C., *A History of the Art of War in the Middle Ages Volume 2 1278–1485* (Greenhill Books, 1991)

Parry, V. J., *A History of the Ottoman Empire to 1730* (Cambridge University Press, 1976)

Vaughan, D. M., *Europe and the Turk: A Pattern of Alliances 1350–1700* (Liverpool University Press, 1954)

Zachariadou, Elizabeth A. (ed.), *Romania and the Turks (c. 1300–1500)* (Variorum Reprints, London, 1985)

Index

Related titles & companion series from Osprey

CAMPAIGN (CAM)
Strategies, tactics and battle experiences of opposing armies

WARRIOR (WAR)
Motivation, training, combat experiences and equipment of individual soldiers

ELITE (ELI)
Uniforms, equipment, tactics and personalities of troops and commanders

MEN-AT-ARMS (MAA)
Uniforms, equipment, history and organisation of troops

FORTRESS (FOR)
Design, technology and history of key fortresses, strategic positions and defensive systems
Contact us for more details – see below

ESSENTIAL HISTORIES (ESS)
Concise overviews of major wars and theatres of war
Contact us for more details – see below

NEW VANGUARD (NVG)
Design, development and operation of the machinery of war
Contact us for more details – see below

To order any of these titles, or for more information on Osprey Publishing, contact:
Osprey Direct (UK) *Tel:* +44 (0)1933 443863 *Fax:* +44 (0)1933 443849 *E-mail:* info@ospreydirect.co.uk
Osprey Direct (USA) c/o MBI Publishing *Toll-free:* 1 800 826 6600 *Phone:* 1 715 294 3345
Fax: 1 715 294 4448 *E-mail:* info@ospreydirectusa.com
www.ospreypublishing.com

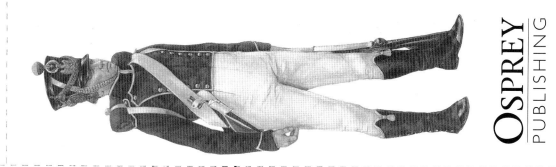

FIND OUT MORE ABOUT OSPREY

❏ Please send me the latest listing of Osprey's publications

❏ I would like to subscribe to Osprey's e-mail newsletter

Title / rank

Name

Address

City / county

Postcode / zip   state / country

e-mail

ESS

I am interested in:

❏ Ancient world
❏ Medieval world
❏ 16th century
❏ 17th century
❏ 18th century
❏ Napoleonic
❏ 19th century

❏ American Civil War
❏ World War 1
❏ World War 2
❏ Modern warfare
❏ Military aviation
❏ Naval warfare

Please send to:

USA & Canada:
Osprey Direct USA, c/o MBI Publishing, P.O. Box 1,
729 Prospect Avenue, Osceola, WI 54020

UK, Europe and rest of world:
Osprey Direct UK, P.O. Box 140, Wellingborough,
Northants, NN8 2FA, United Kingdom

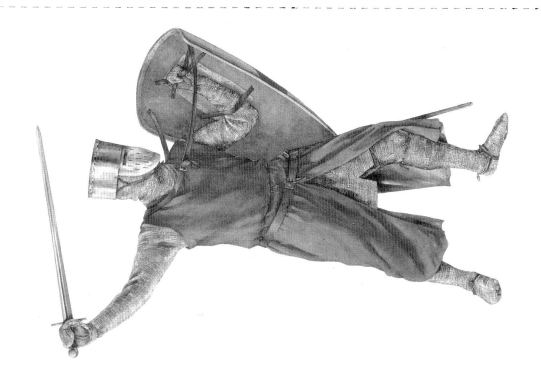

OSPREY
PUBLISHING

www.ospreypublishing.com

call our telephone hotline
for a free information pack

USA & Canada: 1-800-826-6600
UK, Europe and rest of world call:
+44 (0) 1933 443 863

Young Guardsman
Figure taken from *Warrior 22:
Imperial Guardsman 1799–1815*
Published by Osprey
Illustrated by Richard Hook

Knight, c.1190
Figure taken from *Warrior 1: Norman Knight 950 – 1204 AD*
Published by Osprey
Illustrated by Christa Hook

POSTCARD

www.ospreypublishing.com